Domestic Transferable Permits for Environmental Management

DESIGN AND IMPLEMENTATION

OECD

ORGANISATION FOR ECONOMIC CO-OPERATION AND DEVELOPMENT

ORGANISATION FOR ECONOMIC CO-OPERATION AND DEVELOPMENT

Pursuant to Article 1 of the Convention signed in Paris on 14th December 1960, and which came into force on 30th September 1961, the Organisation for Economic Co-operation and Development (OECD) shall promote policies designed:

– to achieve the highest sustainable economic growth and employment and a rising standard of living in Member countries, while maintaining financial stability, and thus to contribute to the development of the world economy;

– to contribute to sound economic expansion in Member as well as non-member countries in the process of economic development; and

– to contribute to the expansion of world trade on a multilateral, non-discriminatory basis in accordance with international obligations.

The original Member countries of the OECD are Austria, Belgium, Canada, Denmark, France, Germany, Greece, Iceland, Ireland, Italy, Luxembourg, the Netherlands, Norway, Portugal, Spain, Sweden, Switzerland, Turkey, the United Kingdom and the United States. The following countries became Members subsequently through accession at the dates indicated hereafter: Japan (28th April 1964), Finland (28th January 1969), Australia (7th June 1971), New Zealand (29th May 1973), Mexico (18th May 1994), the Czech Republic (21st December 1995), Hungary (7th May 1996), Poland (22nd November 1996), Korea (12th December 1996) and the Slovak Republic (14th December 2000). The Commission of the European Communities takes part in the work of the OECD (Article 13 of the OECD Convention).

Publié en français sous le titre :

PERMIS TRANSFÉRABLES NATIONAUX ET POLITIQUES ENVIRONNEMENTALES
Conception et application

Photo Credit:
Jeremy Walker/Stone

Foreword

Further to an OECD workshop on the use of domestic tradable permits as instruments for environmental management (September 1998), it was decided that an in-depth analysis should be made of the conditions applying to the introduction of domestic transferable permit systems. This report therefore provides a systematic analysis of the various approaches, challenges, conditions and potential solutions relating to the design and introduction of tradable permits at the national level. The work was carried out under the supervision of the OECD Working Party on Economic and Environmental Policy Integration.

This report was written by Mr. Olivier Godard, Director of Research at the CNRS, Laboratoire d'Econométrie de l'Ecole Polytechnique (Paris). The book is published under the responsibility of the Secretary-General of the OECD.

Table of contents

List of Boxes

List of Tables

List of Figures

Introduction

Transferable permits (TPs) are a family of policy instruments that are currently attracting growing interest in OECD Member countries. This type of economic instruments covers the full gamut of mechanisms ranging from measures to ease conventional administrative regulatory regimes to the organisation of a competitive and open market for permits. In all instances, the instrument combines two elements:

- the setting of quantified physical constraints in the form of obligations, permits or rights allocated to target-groups (polluting firms, fishermen, land-owners, consumers, etc.);
- the authorisation of such target-groups, under certain conditions specified by an administrative authority, to transfer these obligations, permits or rights either from one activity to other activities controlled by the same agent, from one time period to another, from one geographical area to another, or from the agent in question to other economic agents; these various options can in turn be combined in different ways.

This approach allows decentralised agents to choose the best means of meeting the overall constraint set by the authorities, including the means requiring changes to be made to the distribution of that constraint among themselves. In the case of air pollution, it is therefore the distribution of pollutant emission permits between different sources[1] which decentralised agents can alter by initiating transfers. In the case of natural resources, it is usage or abstraction rights which can be transferred in space or over time, or from one agent to another.

These mechanisms can be applied when the sources in question are placed under the legal control of a given economic agent or that of several agents. In its most advanced form this instrument can lead to the institutional creation of a formal and fully-fledged market for emission permits. However, some schemes commonly classified under the heading of "tradable permits" bear little resemblance to a market or even to the concept of trading if the "external" transactions between separate economic agents plays a negligible role in their implementation. In such cases TPs are best seen as a means of introducing regulatory flexibility more than a market instrument. A good example of this is the concept of "bubbles" in which requirements of pollution abatement are applied to the sources of an industrial facility owned by the same firm, by taking all these sources as a whole. It is for this reason that the generic term "transferable permits" has been used in this study to refer to all possible types of scheme, regardless of whether or not they give rise to commercial transactions.

Despite the above, the main intention of the instrument remains the same. By giving decentralised agents, both singly and collectively, the choice of the means by which an environmental quality or natural resource management objective can be achieved and by exposing agents to the appropriate economic incentives, the community benefits from the best information held by decentralised agents and, if it is assumed that these agents are aware of the potential costs of their activities, from their ability to choose the least expensive solutions without that information having to be communicated to a supervisory authority.

A variety of areas potentially fall within the scope of TPs. Examples include the control of air pollution from stationary sources at different territorial levels, ranging from the prevention of acid rain at the regional level to efforts to curb global warming; the standardisation of product lines responsible for polluting emissions at the stage of consumer use (cars, engines) or of disposal (e.g. CFC in end-of-use refrigerators); efforts to curb water pollution at the local level or along certain rivers; the management of certain natural resources in accordance with ecological or development constraints (irrigation water, sea fisheries, assignment of building rights); to the organisation of recycling systems for industrial and household wastes and packaging wastes in particular. In this regard, TPs provide a tool able to tackle the manifold issues raised by the design of policies for sustainable development. Specifically, TPs can help introducing structural change both in consumption patterns and production technology and organisation by phasing ambitious long run objectives.

Within a period of barely twenty or so years, TPs have thus progressed from the stage of theoretical proposal and initial trials at the local level to that of an instrument used on a large scale by a major country (the United States) and, potentially, that of a major international policy instrument in efforts to curb global warming. This historical development provides some interesting insights. While on the one hand much still remains to be done to expand the scope and focus of efforts to exploit the potential of this instrument, which has not as yet made any tangible inroads into the continents of Europe, Africa and Asia, there is now sufficient distance from the initial experiments to be able to draw certain conclusions that can guide the work of the experts and the administrative and political decision-makers responsible for new developments in environmental policy.

The aim of this study is to consider the principal issues that arise when work starts on designing a TP system within a country and to indicate the parameters and variables that administrative and political decision-makers are recommended to take into account during the design stage. The study seeks to shed light on how these decision-makers can best make use of the potential of the instrument while at the same time taking account of the constraints and conditions that might ultimately affect adoption of the instrument. The discussion will therefore address the competitiveness of firms and the political acceptability of the instrument and will be based as much on the empirical experience that has been gained as on the theoretical work contained in the literature, which has grown substantially over the past twenty-five years. In fact, the experience that will be drawn upon is two-fold in that it covers both completed schemes in which TPs have been put in place and situations in which projects of this type ultimately failed to be implemented, as has been the case in countries as diverse as Switzerland, the United Kingdom and Poland.

The area chosen for discussion is that of environmental protection and the management of natural resources at the local or national level. These two domains have been considered together given the fact that most of the problems posed by the design and implementation of a TP system are the same, even though the solutions eventually adopted may differ.

This study does not address issues relating to the organisation of international TPs such as those which emerged during discussions on the implementation of the Kyoto Protocol (1997) to the Framework Convention on Climate Change. It is simply not possible to address these major and specific issues only by extrapolating practices and rules of the game adopted at national level by a given State to the international level (Hourcade and Baron, 1993). Moreover, these issues have been covered in depth by a dedicated literature relating to, for example, initial quota allocations and burden-sharing, compliance with quantified objectives (choice of implementation mechanisms, potential sanctions) or the core variables that need to be harmonised from one country to another as part of a system of international co-operation. The study does not consider either related schemes such as markets for production quotas put in place for non-environmental reasons such as those introduced to maintain sectoral economic equilibria or to reabsorb structural over-capacities in production, as in the case, for example, of milk quotas in Canada.

The report has been divided into five chapters. The first chapter describes the background to this instrument and the main reasons for making use of it in public policy implementation systems; it then provides basic definitions and describes the main types of TPs. The second chapter provides a systematic review of the all the variables that enter into the design of a TP system by considering in turn the aims and basic characteristics of a programme, options for the design of such a system and, lastly, the means of implementing it. The third chapter addresses the principal issues that inform the choice of such an instrument: the impact on the competitiveness of firms, compatibility with the institutional framework for policy; distributive aspects; the social dimension and lastly political acceptability. The fourth chapter discusses circumstances that might affect the advisability of making use of TPs rather than other instruments. The fifth chapter looks at the considerations which should inform strategic choices with regard to development of a TP system once the decision has been taken to adopt this instrument. It first examines the contents of the instrument and then the management of the process of designing and implementing the instrument.

This analysis was used as a basis for the drafting of "Guidelines for the design and implementation of transferable permits".

Note

1. A source consists in a point, whose location is identified by the administration, at which polluting emissions are released into the environment. A factory chimney or stack is a source, as is an outflow for the release of liquid effluents or a car. An industrial facility usually has several sources. The conventional approach to industrial pollution consists in determining limit-values for each source.

Chapter 1

Origins, Aims and Approaches

Brief Historical Overview[1]

As policy instruments, the transfer of permits or quotas have roots in both theory and practice. The economic theory of pollutant emission markets began to take shape towards the end of the 1960s, following work by Coase (1960) on external costs and Demsetz (1964) on property rights in relation to the use of collective resources. These two avenues of research both pointed towards the idea of using direct bargaining among agents as a means of solving problems, including those relating to collective goods, once the respective property or usage rights had been duly clarified by the State. Since the victims of pollution were either too numerous or unable to take part directly to such transactions (high-level transaction costs), this initial basic concept has evolved into a scheme in which the State represented the focus for demand for environmental services from citizen-consumers matching the demands of good producers. This subsequently led to the idea of organising markets to trade pollutant emission rights responding to public goals. A number of key studies mark this development, notably the pioneering work of Dales (1968*a*) on regulating water use, the paper on air by Crocker (1966) and Montgomery's formal analysis (1972) of markets for pollution and emission permits.

Practical innovation in the area of pollution control came from environmental policy managers in the United States. In the mid 1970s they began to experiment with various forms of flexible regulation to deal with pollution problems, and air pollution in particular. The main issue was to find ways of avoiding a potential bar on further industrial development in areas, chiefly in California, which were failing to achieve the federal government's air quality targets because of the density and rising number of polluting activities (stationary and mobile sources) that accompanied strong economic growth. The idea that emerged was to continue to allow new industry to set up provided it made use of the most effective pollution control technology and could prove that the additional emissions that would ensue would be offset by a reduction in emissions from existing sources. That gave rise to the offset system (Hahn and Hester, 1989).

With the economic repercussions of the 1974 oil shock, finding solutions which would lower the costs to business of complying with environmental regulations, without jeopardising quality targets, also became of concern for the authorities in the United States. That led to the bubble system, pooling the requirements placed on all existing sources in a given facility, industrial zone or small region. A bubble therefore permits higher emissions from some existing sources provided that they are offset by lower emissions from others.

Other forms of spatial and temporal flexibility were introduced and tried out by adjusting the regulatory framework. The common feature in these proposals was that additional pollutant emissions into the atmosphere were allowed from one source over a given period, provided they were offset by what was deemed to be an equivalent reduction in emissions from another source or over another period.

The bulk of these methods reorganised the distribution of regulatory emission permits among a number of sources controlled by one same economic agent. The idea of a market, matching substantial regular volumes of supply and demand from competing agents, was still some distance away. Even though offset arrangements had produced some external transactions during the 1980s, the decisive step towards a market in TPs was taken with the 1990 Clean Air Act Amendments (CAAA). This reform laid the foundation for a market in sulphur dioxide (SO_2) emission allowances extending right across the country, the main mandatory focus being emissions from power stations, many of which burnt coal (Acid Rain Program). The approach was a novel one, setting a national target for SO_2 and NO_x reductions over the 1980 emission levels, as well as a special ceiling for total SO_2 emissions by the electricity generating sector. The latter ceiling was then allocated among power stations in the form of individual quotas that could be freely transferred (Kete, 1992; Howe, 1994; Godard, 1994; Burtraw, 1996; Ellerman *et al.*, 1997; Scharze and Zapfel, 1999).

A number of local experiments with regard to water pollution also took place in the United States – the main subject, in fact, addressed by Dales in his 1968 papers. The first trial was launched in March 1981 in Wisconsin, on a 60 km stretch of the lower Fox River which was receiving effluent from ten pulping mills as well as four towns (O'Neil *et al.*, 1983). Subsequently these experiments were not taken as far as with air pollution, for reasons which will be described further on.

The use of TPs, although commonest now for air pollution, goes back much further with the exploitation or use of some natural resources. There is considerable local experience of trading rights to abstract water in a number of countries, the United States, Australia and Chile in particular (Kraemer and Banholzer, 1999), chiefly to allocate water for irrigation or to strike a balance between farm and non-farm use. Some countries have a long-standing practice of trading rights or quotas for river fishing, and the method has also been tried out at various times for some sea fisheries, whale hunting for instance. The 1932 agreement between British and Norwegian whalers, for example, set catch quotas and limits on the whaling season in Antarctica. From the outset the quotas were meant to be transferable, but no price was set (Tonnessen *et al.*, 1982). A number of countries (Australia, Canada, Iceland, Netherlands, New Zealand, United States) have used this instrument, especially from the 1970s onwards, for a variety of species including tuna, lobster, shrimp, herring and sole (Wallis, 1999). For land-use management and building regulation in areas of exceptional environmental value or for town planning purposes, transferable development rights have been used in the United States since the 1900s, although the most significant applications from an environmental protection standpoint began to appear in the early 1980s (Renard, 1999). In New Zealand the transferable rights method gained prominence from 1974 onwards with the redevelopment plan for central Auckland, the purpose being to safeguard the historical and architectural heritage.

At the international level, the Oslo Protocol to the Geneva Convention on long-range airborne pollution sets quantified reduction objectives for the signatory countries but also establishes the principle that countries may undertake on a voluntary basis to meet their commitments jointly (Bailey and Jackson, 1999; Godard, 1999). More recently, according to the Kyoto Protocol to the Framework Convention on Climate Change, adopted in December 1997 but not as yet ratified, countries that have committed themselves to quantified reductions (QELROS) in six greenhouse gases over the period 2008-2012 may, in accordance with procedures yet to be established, trade the emission quotas which they have accepted to respect; they may also achieve the latter in association with other countries so that they can benefit from emission credits for reductions they might finance in countries that have not committed themselves to a quantified reduction (Godard and Henry, 1998; Skea, 1999). These provisions therefore foreshadow a new type of international trade which, were it to emerge, would amount to the largest TP scheme ever seen.

This short summary shows that TPs or quotas are used to quite different extents depending on the target resource, the type of problem, and the country. But the most significant experiments have taken place since the 1980s.

Aims and Expected Benefits

Four Main Aims

There are four main reasons for the interest shown in TPs. The first objective worth noting is the desire to improve environmental performance and the information obtained on the latter. Expectations addressed to TPs relate both to technical aspects, but also the political economy of instruments:

- TPs directly account for the environmental impacts of human activities through the formulation of quantified objectives or physical constraints related to environmental quality, whereas regulations based on technology alone only provide approximate guarantees regarding environmental impacts;
- This approach also requires strict controls on the observance of these quantified parameters (emissions monitoring) in order to ensure rights on assets that have a market value, unlike regulations which are sometimes only accompanied by sporadic or inadequate controls to ensure that the regulations in force are properly effective;
- In terms of the political economy of the instrument, it is worth noting that it is in the interest of each agent participating in the TP system that others make proper use of their permit allocations since the value of the permits held by each agent depends upon it. With TPs regulated agents receive incentives to be vigilant about ensuring that permits are used properly and that the administrative authorities do not behave in an arbitrary fashion. The same agents might be economically indifferent to poor application of traditional regulations. Moreover non-governmental organisations (NGOs) and the officials of environmental protection agencies are generally extremely keen to be able to obtain precise information on emissions levels from individual sources and also at sectoral or regional levels. To do this, however, the level of cheating or failures in the inspection system must be negligible.

In any case, the interest in acquiring *ex ante* a certainty regarding the physical performance that a policy will achieve at a given date is not always of great importance. That will depend upon the type of problem considered. It may be of great interest in the case of local public health problems, particularly in that no threshold effects can be expected; but it will be of lesser interest in the case of efforts to combat long-term cumulative problems such as the greenhouse effect, whose trend trajectory is more important than specific performance achievements in finding a solution to the environmental problem (Godard, 1993*a*). Nonetheless, the basis on which at some date TPs operate requires that initial rights and subsequent behaviour (in terms of emissions and abstractions) must be precisely monitored, regardless of the interest, *per se*, in securing this information in order to inform the choice of a public policy.

The second reason lies in the flexibility with which policy can be implemented. Not only do TPs increase the range of means available to each decentralised agent to achieve a given environmental objective, but at the level of the local or regional economic fabric they make it possible to avoid the pursuit of environmental protection objectives becoming an impediment to the economic development of an industrial basin. TPs allow a better match to be obtained with the specific individual and collective circumstances in which economic agents conduct their activities.

The third reason is that, of all environmental policy instruments, TPs, or at least the most comprehensive type based on quotas[2], are the only instrument capable of imposing or allowing, depending upon one's point of view, an explicit and separate treatment of distributive aspects[3]. This instrument affords the greatest freedom of choice with regard to a distribution strategy, in terms of both procedures and beneficiaries. If market imperfections and transaction costs are not so high that they become a significant source of disequilibrium (Stavins, 1995), it makes it possible to discriminate between two objectives while at the same time giving them a precise articulation, namely to ensure an economically efficient allocation of the efforts imposed by an environmental objective and to ensure a satisfactory distribution of the income effects with regard to the distributive objectives pursued by the community.

Lastly, the most obvious reason for economists who pay attention to the costs of environmental policy is in terms of economic efficiency. TPs are generally expected to secure a satisfactory economic performance in dealing with new problems or to significantly improve the economic performance of the policies in place. This property is sufficiently important to merit a closer examination of the mechanisms that underpin it.

Expected Economic Benefits

In many cases the scope of decentralised initiatives given to regulated agents, by allowing them to transfer the permits they hold plays a decisive role in reducing the overall economic cost of an approach based on rationing volumes. The economic superiority often claimed for TPs over traditional regulatory approaches lies in the fact that the quantities authorised for one source can be transferred to other sources. This transferability is crucially important from an economic standpoint. It gives rise to an economic mechanism that is radically different to the classical use of regulations, voluntary agreements or even, in certain cases, subsidies[4]. This is because it confers a general opportunity cost on the use of permits by the holders of those permits. Any available permit could provide an economic benefit or income if it were used for another use controlled by the agent or sold to another agent, as is the case with any other market asset. With fully developed market of TPs, the opportunity cost is set by the market value of permits.

Consideration of this opportunity cost by economic agents when making production and technology decisions tends to equalise the marginal costs of pollution abatement to which agents are exposed, or the marginal value derived from natural resources by the various agents involved in their exploitation. It tends to align the allocative effect of TPs on that of an incentive tax: the equilibrium price in a competitive market for TPs will be of the same value as the tax needed to achieve the same cut in emissions. It will reflect the social value of the scarcity created by the government's physical rationing of pollution.

This basic mechanism is illustrated in Figure 1 below, which actually deals with pollution although a similar chart could be produced for use of a rationed physical resource.

The magnitude of the cost reduction depends on the context in which the mechanism is applied in practice; it may range from 10 to 95% (Tietenberg, 1992). In the US Acid Rain Program, a fully developed market could reduce costs by a factor of 3 (Burtraw, 1996). While actual savings are hard to estimate (problems of imputation and in constructing a counterfactual reference), they could nonetheless reach 30% for the first year (1995) of the binding enforcement of the programme (Ellerman *et al.*, 1997).

This property of economic efficiency is achieved at best if there is no bias introduced into the mechanism through fiscal disparities and other market imperfections. Arbitrary differences in taxes, such as excise duties, that *a priori* can create distortions, may have an adverse impact on the operation of TP schemes by inducing transfers that run counter to those which normally would enhance economic efficiency (see Box 1). Such a limit is not specific to TPs. Biases of a similar nature, in terms of their eventual outcome, can also affect incentive taxes or conventional regulatory schemes, would these instruments be applied to economic agents exposed to distorted market conditions.

On this economic side of the distribution of efforts to control pollution or rights to use a natural resource, TPs are held to have a number of additional advantages:

- The formation of transfer prices that are made publicly known and that, as they approach a competitive market price, provide valuable information to all decentralised economic agents; while it does not dispel all uncertainty regarding how such information should be interpreted in economic terms, TPs offer the major advantage of bringing economic objectivity to expert controversies about the right economic assessment. Differences of opinion of experts are often

Figure 1. **50 per cent Reduction in Emissions (after Godard and Henry, 1998)**

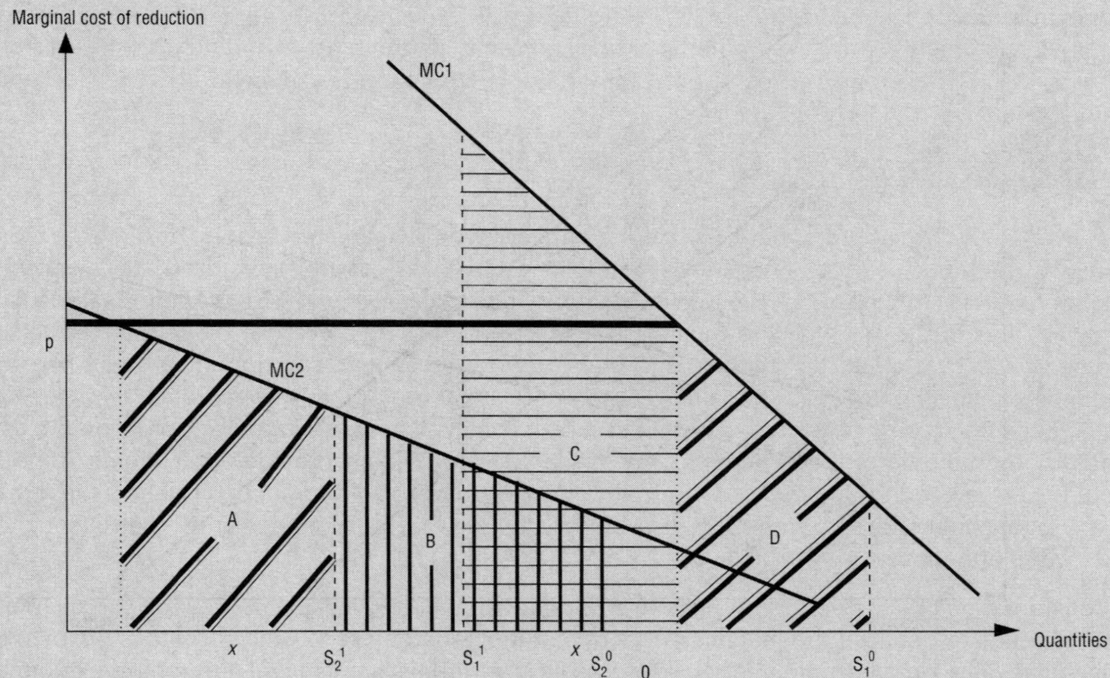

Two sources S_1 and S_2 have emission levels S_1^0 and S_2^0, before any requirement to cut emissions, and each have a portfolio of cutback options whose costs are shown by the marginal cost of reduction functions MC1 and MC2. With a uniform target of a 50 % reduction, S_1 has to bear a total cost shown by area C + D, to achieve level S_1^1, and source S_2 has to bear a cost represented by area B to achieve level S_2^1. The corresponding allocation (S_1^1, S_2^1) involves unnecessarily high total costs, reflecting the very different marginal costs (in the ratio of 1 to 2 in the chart). For the parties concerned and for the community as a whole, the allocation could be improved by reducing total costs for the same overall abatement target. That is possible via a mechanism for trading the quotas covering the uniform 50 % reduction. In satisfactory conditions (for instance, no information asymmetry), transactions should reach equilibrium at price ***p***. By cutting its emissions by a further x units, S_2 obtains surplus emission permits which it can sell on to S_1, which restricts its own abatement effort accordingly and so reduces costs. In all, S_1 now bears a net cost equal to D + ***px*** and S_2 a net cost of B + A – ***px***. Total cost B + D + C is reduced to B + D + A, with A < C.

Box 1. **Impact of Asymmetries on Tax Treatment**

Let us take the case of two agents holding TPs whose activities are subject to differing fiscal regulations because the two agents operate in different sectors or categories. The table of costs including taxes for the two agents may give rise to transfers which run counter to those leading to an increase in overall economic efficiency. The reason for this is that abating emissions is also a means to abate variable taxes based on inputs or outputs complementary to emissions. For instance, the agent whose marginal costs before tax are higher than those of the other agent, but who is also subject to higher taxation, would nonetheless be encouraged to step up his efforts to reduce pollution more than required by the optimum allocation so that he can buy less permits to the other or even he can sell a share of his permits to the other whose costs before tax are lower but whose tax burden is also lower. The obvious benefits of such a transaction for both of the agents concerned would therefore be more than offset by the loss of income to the State and subsequently that of tax-payers and consumers. Incidentally, this interference of differences in tax treatment will change the equilibrium (price, quantities) on the permit market (Figure 2).

Figure 2. **The Impact of Differences of Taxation of Inputs Linked to Emissions**

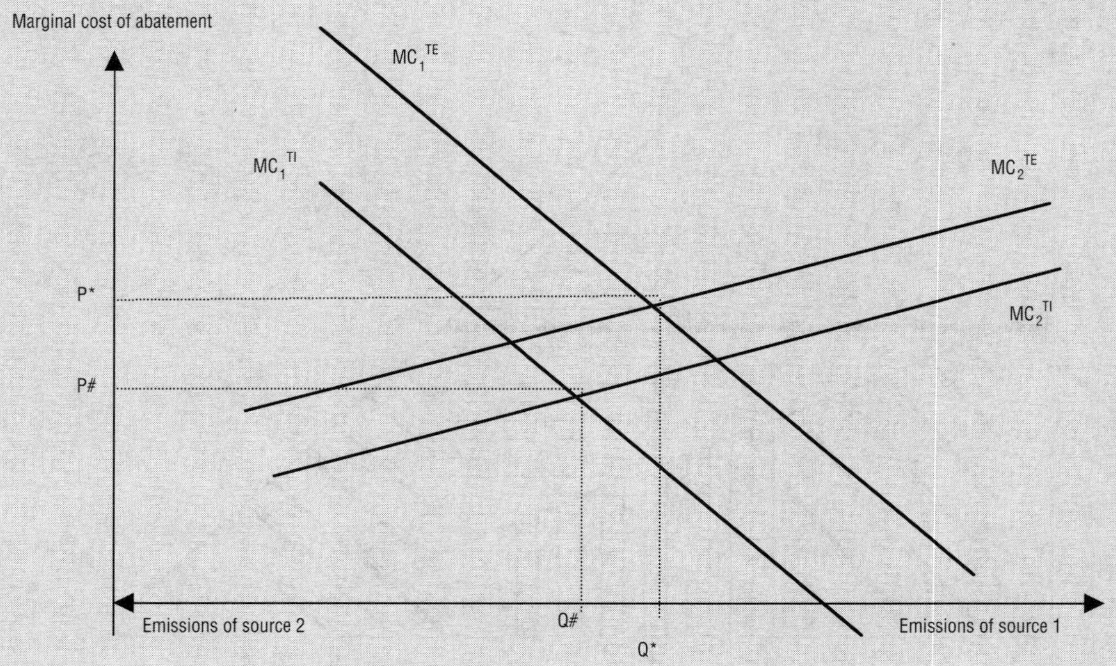

Sources 1 and 2 have marginal abatement costs before any consideration of taxation MC_1^{TE} and MC_2^{TE}. This leads to an optimal allocation of abatement efforts resulting from trading defined by (P*, Q*). But emissions being linked to the consumption of some inputs and these inputs being submitted to different tax regimes between Source 1 and 2, net private abatement costs are reduced in a different proportion by the amount of gain on input taxes. Although marginal costs before trading are higher for Source 1 than for Source 2, the gain in saving taxes is also higher for Source 1 than for Source 2. The market equilibrium leads to an equilibrium (P#, Q#) which implies more abatement effort from Source 1 than is socially optimal. The permit market is affected by differences in tax regimes of complementary goods.

used by interest groups to gain strategic advantage in their efforts to influence the policy process, introducing confusion and sometimes an extravagant lack of realism as a result. Public disclosure of a market equilibrium price is an essential factor in the proper functioning of a decentralised economy. Because other policy instruments do not possess this property, they are more exposed to informational bias and to the use of economic expertise as a weapon by interest groups;

- *The creation of a permanent individual incentive to hold pollution down below the level set by government*, as the extra effort can yield revenue via the sale of unused rights. TPs, like incentive taxation, are said to encourage technological advance. That effect has not been empirically demonstrated in the experiments to hand, on account of the numerous factors involved in decisions to modernise production. Meanwhile TPs have enabled agents to take advantage of fairly rapid and unexpected changes in the institutional environment (deregulation of transport, for example) and the technological environment (technology of pollution control such as filtering);

- Automatic adjustment of the instrument and the behaviour of decentralised agents in response to changes in the general economic context (inflation, growth, higher demand for resources and environmental amenities), without the need for a policy decision or a new administrative measure: the economic conditions under which transfers are made (price formation) provides a decentralised means of inducing the adjustments required by the new scarcity conditions with regard to permits and other economic goods. This property makes the instrument particularly attractive for countries moving towards a market economy whose macroeconomy environment has not yet stabilised (Zylicz, 1999), even though other factors (inoperative legal system, corruption) weaken the instrument's force in that context (Godard, 1995*a*);

- The absence of a financial shock to firms with systems of emission credits or in the event of initial permits being allocated without charge in quota systems. Although the allocation of permits free of charge is often challenged by those parties outside the business world, it has proved to be a politically attractive option for the firms who benefit from in that it allows them to appropriate a share[5] of the scarcity rent arising from the imposition of a given level of environmental constraint. They may even gain a competitive advantage, in terms of profitability or entry barriers in the case of imperfect competition on the product market, over new entrants if the latter have to buy all the permits that they require[6]. Free allocation was the course taken in the United States with the Acid Rain Program. It also underpins the proposals, which were backed by business circles, to introduce TPs in Norway, first of all for SO_2 and more recently CO_2 (Schreiner, 1999).

There are therefore major points in favour of TPs if the use of this instrument is compared with conventional regulatory approaches. They are not the only ones, however, since there are also environmental or political benefits that can be expected of TPs. The latter may have a critical importance for the political acceptance of this sort of instrument.

Basic Definitions and Concepts

Four Main Families of Transferable Permit

In the pollution abatement field, specialists usually distinguish two major families of TPs: quotas (*allowances, cap and trade*) and credits (*baseline and credit*) for reducing emissions. There are also a further two families. The first relates to the management of natural resources and consists in the clarification and separating-out of the components of user or ownership rights over natural assets (water, fish, land) so that they can subsequently be transferred (user and property rights). The second relates to a type of regulatory flexibility with regard to products which is termed *averaging*.

So four families of TPs can be isolated. They consist of the following. **Quotas** (*cap and trade* or *minimum limits and trade*) correspond to quantified maxima or minima assigned to agents for a given period. Individual maxima and minima are determined by setting an overall volume (a cap) for a delimited area to which the system applies for a given period. An example of a quantified maximum is the maximum annual volume of sulphur dioxide emissions from power plants on U.S. soil following the enactment of the 1990 CAAA. An example of minimum obligations is provided by the minimum recycling rates for materials contained in packaging wastes currently in force in the European Union[7]. Quotas can be transferred by agents *ex ante* as soon as they have been allocated. Advance transactions may also take place if future rights are clearly defined from the outset of the programme. Compliance with the rules applicable to permit holdings is checked *ex post*.

Emission reduction credits (*baseline and credit for emission reduction*) correspond to the acknowledgement at the end of the period of the achievement of an emission or abstraction level below the one which had been authorised for a given agent over a given period; the reference situation is generally defined by the pre-existing regulatory requirements but may also consists of agreed future prospects for business development; credits are generally granted *ex post* once the performance achieved has been duly confirmed, although it is conceivable to acknowledge them *ex ante* when future performance can be predicted with certainty (for instance from the outset of a change in technology).

Averaging consists in the competent authority setting average limit values for an entire range of similar products (e.g. cars or engines) manufactured by firms within the same industrial branch. Firms then have the option of exceeding these limit values for some of the products they sell on the market provided that these overshoots are offset by higher than average performance levels with regard to other products. Equivalences are calculated by taking account of the respective product volumes of the different models sold, average conditions of use and the expected lifetime of each model. Transfers can also be made externally, i.e. if the overall product performance of a firm is higher than the average performance level prescribed, the firm can transfer its unused permits to another firm whose performance is poorer. An approach of this kind was adopted in the CAFE (*Corporate Average Fuel Economy*) programme designed to regulate the unit consumption of the vehicles sold by automobile manufacturers in the United States.

The attribution of ***transferable usage rights or rights to abstract natural resources*** (*transferable rights*) aims to formally regulate access to resources that are freely available, to organise the regulation of the use of resources whose ownership is shared or, in the case of building and construction rights, to mitigate or compensate impact for owners of the private property restrictions imposed for the sake of environmental protection and sustainable development objectives. Transferable fishing rights and transferable construction rights separated from land ownership rights are two examples of the adoption of such an approach in a country like New Zealand.

The distinctions between these four families do not primarily lie in differences between types of spatial and temporal flexibility, nor in the conditions applicable to transactions, nor, more directly, in the way in which the market operates, but further upstream in the way in which transferable units are determined and allocated. They consist in four different ways of introducing flexibility to government's approach to environmental policy. Quotas are part of a policy approach focusing not on government steering of ways and means but on government setting the targets for improving environmental quality, opening up much wider perspectives of initiative to economic agents. The latter can thus select their strategies without government interfering in their technological decisions, and make use *ex ante* of the opportunities afforded by external transactions.

The credits approach to emissions reduction and averaging fits an overall technological approach of pollution control by government, and hence corresponds rather more to the idea of regulatory flexibility. These approaches have no overall ceiling but use specific regulatory benchmarks for each source identified by government. Generally external transactions only take place *ex post* once emissions can be proved to have been reduced below the limit values imposed. From an environmental standpoint, and given that some parties have reservations about business compliance with quotas, the credits approach clearly holds out greater security, but it does require a more time-consuming and expensive administrative procedure to determine the credits that a source may qualify for. It does, however, entail less initial institutional investment in devising an overall system by government, since it relates directly to the system of administrative permits for existing facilities. In particular, it does not call for an overall ceiling to be defined, or for any general procedure for the initial allocation of permits. But the benchmarks against which credits may be determined need to be clearly defined. A case-by-case procedure will be used to set the credits for which a firm qualifies in respect of a given period. The approach thus maintains strong government control over economic agents and incurs significant transaction costs in terms of time, bargaining costs and uncertainty over outcomes, not to mention the potential sources of conflict it creates for disputes between business, environmental NGOs and government.

Specifying new user and ownership rights forms part of an approach recognising the damage generated by free access to scarce natural resources, and clarifying the individual rights of agents. For some authors, the outcome should be a major extension of individual ownership at the expense of various forms of common or collective ownership (Falque and Massenet, 1997). For others, traditional or modern forms of common ownership may provide wholly effective regimes for natural resource management, in particular with such complex objectives as protecting biodiversity, once a number of rules have been adopted and an organisation is responsible for enforcing them (Ostrom, 1990; Gadgil and Rao, 1994).

The characteristics of the four families of permits are summarised in Table 1.

Table 1. **Credits, Quotas, Averaging and New Rights**

	Credits	Quotas	Averaging	Usage or abstraction rights
Basic concept	Baseline and credit	Cap and trade or minimum limits and trade	Averaging of product requirements	Setting individual property or user rights
Physical basis	Reductions below an agreed baseline	Total number of permits	The entire product range of a firm	Resource use on the basis of free access or common property
What can be transferred	Only credits for reductions, defined in absolute terms	Permits are transferable in full	Internal compensation applies to the total number of permits resulting from application of the limit values. External transfers cannot exceed the net reduction below the average limit values	Different components of rights can be transferred separately
Allocation	Credits are created by the difference between actual performance and an agreed baseline. They can be observed *ex post* or assigned *ex ante* if they are perfectly predicted	Quotas are allocated by a public authority in the form of quantified minima or maxima	wAverage limit values are set by an administrative authority. The volume of TPs depends upon the production level for each product in the range	Rights are defined by a public authority or a local community
Relationship with the regulatory regime	May be phased in as a way of introducing flexibility into an existing regulatory system	Provision must be made for the introduction of transferable quotas into a regulatory system from the outset	May be phased in progressively as a means of introducing flexibility into a product standardisation regime	May be developed on the basis of traditional systems of resource use or as a substitute for them
Conditions of participation	Voluntary: sources can simply comply with the baseline requirements without asking for credits to be validated	Mandatory in that the specified minima and maxima must be complied with even if the sources do not make transfers. Possible provisions for opting-in options or voluntary early programmes	Mandatory. Compliance with regulatory requirements depends upon the average performance of products in the range. Participation in external transfers is voluntary	Mandatory in that the new rights are binding on all parties
Examples	The U.S. federal offset programme to control local air pollution requires new sources to obtain credits from other existing sources	The Acid Rain programme in the United States includes an annual maximum emissions level for the power generating sector, individual allowances and a national perimeter within which quotas can be traded	The mobile source emissions programme in the United States. From 1998 onwards every manufacturer of boat engines must reduce total hydrocarbon releases from new engines sold on the market by 75% over a period of 9 years.	In New Zealand there are transferable individual quota schemes for 33 species of fish

The first two columns are based on the work of Sorrell and Skea (1999, p. 11)

Different Forms of Flexibility

Flexibility over Time

Flexibility over time can be organised in four different ways:

- ***Budgeting*** of emissions or abstractions over a given period of time (quarterly, annual, five-yearly, etc.) during which transfers may be made freely;
- ***Banking***, which consists in authorising the transfer of permits valid for a given period of time to a later period or periods;
- ***Borrowing***, which consists in authorising the advance use of permits that are valid for a given future period; this facility may be restricted in terms of the volume that can be borrowed or the imputation of a cost in a form equivalent to that of an interest rate;

- Differentiation between normal operating regimes and ***short-term periods of pollution peak management***, which bring different adjustment variables and constraints into play. The introduction of special rules for transfers made during these exceptional periods may help to minimise costs. Transfers would have to be made almost instantaneously, however, which would all plea for electronic communications and transactional procedures, and without prior authorisation.

It may be noted that the budgeting approach for emissions over a given period of time amounts to the same thing as authorising permits to be freely banked and borrowed during that period.

Spatial Flexibility

There are three main ways in which flexibility can be achieved in spatial terms: ***emission bubbles, deposition bubbles*** and ***offsets***. Hybrid schemes and other combinations are also feasible.

An emission bubble consists of a designated territorial area embracing a number of sources for which a total emissions ceiling is specified for a given period of time. Once the various sources have received their initial allocation of this quota, they may freely transfer their shares between themselves provided that the ceiling for the bubble is never exceeded. In practice, the size of bubbles can vary according to the type of environmental problem concerned; a bubble can apply to a given industrial facility, industrial basin, region, industrial sector or country.

A deposition bubble applies to all sources whose emissions give rise to depositions at a given target area within a country, on the basis of a system which Montgomery (1972) felt offered great potential. These sources may not be in close territorial proximity. A limit value is set for total permissible deposition at that point. This total is then used as a basis for distributing deposition permits between the various sources concerned. Permits can then be transferred from one source to another, provided that they comply with the requirements applicable to the permits held by these sources for other points of deposition. The principle on which this system is based is as follows. First, the authorities select a number of deposition points that are representative of the pollution problems affecting the area concerned. The number of deposition bubbles corresponds to the number of points selected. Permits are given for each deposition bubble, so that a permit valuable for one bubble cannot be used for another one. A given source can hold a portfolio of deposition permits for the various local deposits arising from its emissions. Each permit within that portfolio may be transferred to sources having deposition at the corresponding deposition bubble.

Offset schemes provide for transfers between several bubbles, whose individual ceilings are adjusted accordingly. The differences in the stringency of the environmental constraints relating to each bubble are reflected in a variety of restrictions on transfers: asymmetrical rights between the positions of buyers and vendors or between new and existing facilities; setting of offset rates which lay down the specific terms under which emission permits for different bubbles can be traded. For example, an offset rate of 1.5 would mean that an agent located in Bubble A must have acquired a permit for 1.5 units from a source located in Bubble B in order to be entitled to emit 1 additional unit in Bubble A.

Netting as Transfers of Regulatory Regimes

Netting schemes are a variation on a bubble at the level of an industrial facility. They are primarily designed not to permit spatial or temporal transfers of emission permits but rather to introduce flexibility into the change of regulatory regime normally applicable to a facility. They consist in combining the application of overall requirements for that facility with rules for exceptions to a given regulatory status.

Besides the US *netting* programme (see Box 2), other examples of this kind may be found in urban land-use management, when waivers are granted for occupation or density coefficients in exchange for counterparts taking the form, for instance, of funding for facilities which enhance the standard of urban services. Such transactions, which come to negotiating the implementation of a regulation, are fairly distinct from the idea of a market or spatial transfer of construction rights from one plot to another (Renard, 1999).

Clearly netting is the type of flexibility that is furthest removed from the market concept in that there are no transactions between distinct economic agents; the spatial transfer of permits, where applicable, remains confined to the perimeter of a facility. It is therefore a scheme which aptly illustrates how flexibility can be introduced into enforcement of a regulatory regime.

Box 2. **The Netting Programme in the United States**

Introduced in the 1970s, this scheme is based on the following rule: an existing facility that wishes to increase its capacity or modernise existing plant undergoes a change of regulatory regime; instead of benefiting from the less stringent limit values reserved for existing facility, they become subject to the stricter conditions imposed on new facilities. The *netting* programme introduced scope for waivers: modernised plant may continue to be treated under the existing facility regime if the resulting additional emissions incurred are adequately offset by reductions at existing sources so that the net level of any additional emissions is below the threshold for compliance with the industrial pollution control regime. This method has been widely used and accounts for the bulk of the cost savings achieved in the United States during the pioneering period of TPs (1977-1990) (Hahn and Hester, 1989*a* and *b*).

Notes

1. An analysis of recent experiences is provided in OECD (1999) "Implementing Domestic Tradable Permits for Environmental Protection".
2. Solely approaches based on quotas or usage rights, which require an initial allocation stage, have this property. This is not the case of approaches based on credits and averaging which are based on technical references.
3. For an explanation of the differences between issues relating to economic efficiency and those relating to distribution see Chapter 3, page 69 below.
4. Of course, when government subsidises each unit reduction in pollution, continuing to pollute has an opportunity cost, namely the subsidy foregone. But when a one-off subsidy is offered for investment contributing to lower emissions, the firm receiving the subsidy has no incentive to select the most economical methods to cut its pollution: once the subsidy has been obtained, spending it has no opportunity cost for the firm, which cannot use it for a purpose other than the one advanced to obtain the subsidy.
5. The sharing-out of the scarcity rent associated with an environmental objective is governed by the share of the effort imposed without compensation on regulated agents (limits of fishing days; rate of pollution abatement, etc.) and the size of the efficiency gains over a usual administrative regulatory approach achieved through transfers. If the objective is not, on the whole, very costly to achieve, but the trading gains are high due to highly contrasting individual situations, the rent appropriated by permit beneficiaries may be high.
6. In context of rather competitive markets, the current conditions of competition between existing facilities and new comers is not to be significantly affected by the asymmetry in initial access to permits, since the same opportunity cost imposes itself as a benchmark to all agents. But respective investment capacities may be affected in a longer range. On this point, see later in Chapter 3, page 55. With imperfect competition, existing firms may take advantage of free access to permits in order to adopt price policies that dissuade new entrance.
7. The minima specified in the directives currently in force have not yet been used as a basis for organising TPs in Europe. This could be a major field of development for the use of TPs in this region.

Chapter 2

Key Variables in the Design of a Transferable Permits System

Designing a TP system can be likened to a sequential decision-making process involving options relating to a number of key variables. Obviously not all potential combinations are feasible in practice. For example, choosing an emission credits approach, based on the regulatory requirements in force, will preclude the use of an auction procedure for the allocation of credits. Different schemes will therefore emerge in accordance with the specific aims of a programme.

It makes practical sense, as suggested by Harrison (1999), to divide variables into three main groups: those dealing with the aims and distinctive characteristics of the action programme; those relating to variations in the design of the TP system; and lastly those dealing with the means deployed to put the system into practice.

Aims and Basic Characteristics of the System

Aims

The objectives assigned to TPs are expressed in somewhat different terms in papers on the economic theory and papers describing actual trials and reflecting the practical intentions of the instrument's promoters. The theoretical literature focuses largely on aspects to do with efficient use of scarce resources, such as minimising total costs for all economic agents and encouraging technical innovation, and analyses permit trading in terms of genuine market operation, ideally entailing extensive matching of supply and demand through the creation of new property rights[1]. The practical writings are more concerned with selecting instruments for various significant economic policy objectives, such as not impeding activity in a given region, placing more responsibility on business and increasing its scope to operate flexibly while complying with regulations, reducing arbitrary government intervention, cutting financial burdens on business or avoiding some distributive effects of other economic instruments such as taxes. These approaches are not incompatible, but present somewhat different facets: what the theoretical literature sees as a market instrument, the empirical writings regard primarily as a more flexible administrative tool than traditional *command-and-control* methods.

TPs can be used to achieve a wide variety of empirical objectives:

- Organise a long-term effort to reduce emissions of different types of global or interregional pollutants such as CO_2 or SO_2 by searching for the cheapest solution and by encouraging technological innovation, while maintaining the ability of agents (firms, consumers) to pursue their activities (production of cement, electricity, car trips, building heating, etc.);
- Curb over-fishing which in cases where modern technology is used tends to occur when free access is granted to fish stocks, while at the same time ensuring that fishing rights are distributed in an equitable and economically viable manner;
- Organise, over a given period of time, the withdrawal of an industrial product such as CFCs or lead in petrol, while at the same time taking account of the consequences on industry of this withdrawal and the uneven ability of different types of producers to adapt their output

accordingly; the flexibility afforded by TPs in such cases precludes the need to align regulatory requirements on those agents whose difficulties are the greatest;

- Manage local water quality improvement schemes in a given drainage basin or stretch of river in cases where there are several sources emitting equivalent forms of pollution in terms of their environmental impact;
- Manage local pollution peaks according to health objectives, while letting room for an economic rationalisation of measures temporarily needed to reduce levels of activity;
- Implement town planning and preserve the natural environment without challenging the right to own real estate but by separating out the right to build and making that right transferable; in such cases TPs are expected to ensure both the efficient allocation of building work and the distribution of real estate rents on what is considered to be an equitable basis.

All of the above examples clearly show that the aims of a given programme contain a mix of three different components: (a) achieving a given result with regard to the environment or the management of natural resources; (b) paying attention to the economic implications of the policy designed to achieve this result, in order to maintain sound activities to the greatest extent possible and reduce the costs imposed on society; (c) ensuring the equitable distribution of rights, efforts, rents and the advantages afforded by the programme. The respective importance of these three considerations varies according to individual circumstances and in some cases only two will be taken into account in the design of the programme. For example, if considerations relating to economic efficiency seem to be of major importance with regard to a given problem and if treating the distributive aspects explicitly would appear crucial, a TP system would be quite appropriate. Certain programmes designed to reduce fishing capacity are therefore primarily aimed at cutting back over-investment and at increasing the income of fishermen by avoiding a too widely spread rent, and have no particular environmental objectives at all[2]. Unfavourable conditions from an efficiency standpoint can nevertheless be in favour of TPs for distributive motives. Redistribution of rents extracted from rights may be the main goal of a TP programme (case of building rights). As a general rule, however, it is important for those responsible for drawing up a TP programme to bear these three aspects in mind and to pay attention to ways in which they might interact or interfere with each other.

Permit Components

Permits are transferable, not physical volumes per se. These permits confer rights and obligations on those who hold them. The contents of these rights and obligations must be clearly specified and in particular the following aspects: the physical basis; the contents of usage rights; the conditions applicable to the exercise of transfer rights; the legal status of permits.

Physical Basis of Permits

The physical components on which permits are based must be very precisely specified. This specification must meet four constraints: (a) components must be linked as directly as possible to the environmental or resource management objective chosen; (b) they must be homogeneous or incorporate agreed equivalences between disparate elements to ensure that can readily be traded; (c) they must be capable of being measured or estimated in a precise and verifiable way, not only by the agent owning the good but also by an inspection authority; (d) they must have spatial and temporal attributes that provide the best match between the individual requirements in terms of the flexibility of transfers between agents, the economic security of agents owning rights and the adaptability of policy.

The main alternatives may be ranked according to several criteria:

- *The input variable taken into account*: depositions, emissions, abstractions, capacities;
- *The unit of measurement*: the basis may be defined in absolute (x tonnes) or relative terms (unit rate of effluent concentration, unit rate of emission per unit of time);

- *The uniformity of the physical basis considered*: the physical flows considered may be of uniform chemical composition, such as SO_2 or CO_2, or may consist of composites such as NO_x and volatile organic compounds (VOC); an attempt might even be made to draw up equivalences between different categories of chemical emission in cases where this would be a more appropriate way of solving given environmental problems.

Choosing from this wide variety of criteria clearly requires a mix based upon the type of environmental problem considered (is it possible to establish scientific equivalences between the impacts of different types of pollutant? do environmental impacts relate to flow intensity or total amounts?), the choice of objectives (should priority be given to safeguarding a given environmental goal or the economic security of agents?), the range of potential options for adaptation (a wide variety of solutions argue in favour of a system centred on emissions or abstractions, whereas limited or zero variety would argue in favour of the regulation of capacities or levels of activity) and the scope for making measurements (what can actually be measured?).

The prevention of environmental damage caused by acid rain clearly illustrates the potential conflict between points (a) (link with the environmental objective) and (c) (possibility of measuring phenomena) above. Ideally, to the extent that the damage depends on the precise location of acid rain depositions, it is the place where pollutants are deposited that should serve as a basis for permits. However, the operational complexities of this solution may lead to preference being given to an emissions-based approach, which is easier for emitters to control and for the supervisory authority to verify, although there is no accurate and sure way of determining the territorial outcome in terms of deposits. This was the solution adopted by the US authorities in the *Acid Rain Program*.

The choice of physical basis may also involuntarily have an adverse impact on the incentives provided by the regulatory system, as shown by the history of regulatory policy in the fishing sector (Box 3).

Box 3. **Attempts to Regulate Overfishing**

The history of fishing regulatory policy reveals the many different forms of trial and error possible in the search for the best way to introduce a constraint into a system of activities. Virtually all possible schemes have been used: restrictions on fishing technology (size of vessels and types of nets), authorised fishing days, periods during which fish can be harvested, amount of fish landed, amount of fish caught. Each of these solutions can encourage forms of behaviour that are contrary to the goals pursued.

For example, regulating the number of days on which vessels could fish resulted in over-investment in powerful, modern boats which were capable of making large catches within a short period of time but which lay idle outside the periods when fishing was permitted. Regulating the volume of fish landed encourages fishermen to sort their catch on-board and to discard fish of lower commercial value, without there being any ready means of detection. Such practices nonetheless add to the demographic pressure on the species concerned, the most potent symbol of which being the dolphin deaths attributable to the tuna fishing industry before new measures could be introduced.

Contents of Usage Rights

According to the basis adopted, certain aspects of the usage rights arising from permits need to be specified. Firstly, permits must be assigned to a given source or economic entity since the permit allows its holder to comply with regulatory obligations that may have different specifications regarding the decision units: firms, plants or sources. Secondly, rights must be expressed either as rights to absolute volumes or simply as relative values. Two different cases have to be considered. In the first one, permits are defined in terms of shares of a quota of emissions or resource availability over a given period of time, with the total quota available being set by a supervisory authority for each new period. By assumption, individual rights remain compatible with the total cap, the value of which is a common constraint for all agents. In the second case, permits are defined in relative terms, framed in echo to a concern for an efficient technological performance, but do not incorporate absolute limits for a given period. Then individual rights of emission or abstraction are defined as the product of a unit value and an activity index for the period of concern. Activity index is an individual variable which is measured *ex post*, at the end of each period. This approach is often used in credit TP systems. To the extent that individual rights depend on specific individual variables the knowledge of which is only obtained *ex post*, the approach does not provide strong *ex ante* guarantees to meet a given overall absolute target.

The choice between these options raises two major questions: who should bear the economic uncertainty between firms, government and consumers and what means of intervention are available to the public regulator? In a system of quotas established in absolute terms and allocated at the beginning of the first period, the ultimate uncertainty over the proper level of rationing is borne by the community; for instance a public body must every year sell or buy quotas to adjust the actual overall quota to the desirable annual ceiling. It is for this reason that, for phenomena that can vary significantly from one period to another, it may be difficult to assign to agents permits established in absolute values when the constraints can change from one period to the next. This may arise in the case of biological phenomena (dynamics of fish populations), the availability of natural resources (water available through rainfall) or peaks in pollution in a given industrial basin. In such cases it might make more sense to define permits in terms of shares of an overall cap over a given period of time (see Box 4). Credit systems raise a different case. Deciding whether the physical basis should be expressed in absolute or in relative terms looms large in the debate over how to combat airborne industrial pollution, the level of which depends upon not only the technology in use but also the usage rate of plant and thus the economic climate in a given sector. A basis expressed in absolute terms offers the community a guarantee that an overall ceiling will be respected, but places the onus of adjustment to unexpectedly varying levels of activity on firms, whereas a basis expressed in relative terms (for example a rate of emissions per unit of output) increase rights allocated to firms in proportion of the development of their business and transfers the uncertainty and cost of adjustment to the public authorities and, beyond them, other economic agents (firms of other sectors, consumers and taxpayers), if it is required that the total emissions level remains below an overall ceiling. This may generate huge differences in ten years or so (see Box 5).

The permits assigned may be valid for a given period or given number of periods – in which case they are comparable to a rental or a leasing contract – or they may be valid indefinitely, in which case they are comparable to property rights. They may apply solely to a given period, or they may be transferred through banking or borrowing. The issue of the temporal profile of permits depends upon the objective constraints, but also upon policy considerations that may be contradictory (see Box 6). One solution is to allocate annual quotas which are valid solely for the year in which they are issued, but

Box 4. **Setting Quotas in Absolute or Relative Terms to Regulate Overfishing**

The authorities can assign to fishermen shares in an annual quota for catches of different species. Every year, the authorities set the annual quota for the subsequent period on the basis of the most recent information available regarding trends in fish stocks. There has been much discussion within the fishing sector as to whether it is better to allocate absolute quotas or percentages of an annual ceiling on authorised catches. Absolute quotas were the solution initially adopted by New Zealand until that country switched to an approach based on set percentages of an annual ceiling in view of the financial burden on the public purse when the government subsequently had to intervene in order to buy back quotas in excess of the annual desirable ceiling (Pearse, 1992). In a system based on shares, the economic value of rights is less secure for the owners since the costs of adjustment are placed on the shoulders of fishing vessel operators; on the other hand, this solution ensures that they have a vested interest in the success of the resource management programme because regeneration of the resource will enhance their potential gains.

Box 5. **Impact of Targets in Relative Units on Uncertainty of Emission Levels**

Consider an industry having an annual output growth rate that can be of 1.5% or 3.0%. In the context of a 12 year abatement programme, this industry claims to be assigned relative emission targets taking account of a 1.0% annual rate of efficiency improvement in emissions and to get credits for any better performance. It is possible to simulate the quantitative impacts of such assumptions on emissions level at terminal year of the programme and the differences in credits obtained by this industry.

Rate of output growth	Relative emissions efficiency targets	Efficiency performance	Emissions in year 12 (100 in year 0)	Credits in year 12
3%	1.0%	1.0%	126.4	–
3%	1.0%	1.5%	118.9	7.5
3%	1.0%	2.0%	111.9	14.5
1.5%	1.0%	1.0%	106	–
1.5%	1.0%	1.5%	99.7	6.3
1.5%	1.0%	2.0%	93.8	12.2

The idea of this simulation has been inspired by a similar exercise by Zapfel (2000).

This table shows several results: (a) in most cases efficiency improvements do not counterbalance the impact of output growth on absolute emissions, which may increase by nearly 27% in 12 years; (b) output growth has a dominant influence on emissions: a difference of 1.5% in growth rate ends-up with a variation of 20% of absolute emissions; with targets defined in relative terms, uncertainty on future economic growth undermines the capability to meet an absolute cap; (c) the greater the output growth and the efficiency performance, the greater is the number of credits obtained that can be transferred and used by other agents: with that system, economic growth and technological progress do not benefit to the environment.

Box 6. **Duration of Permits and Fisheries Regulation**

The need to involve fishermen in the long-term conservation of fish stocks argues in favour of assigning a fishing right of long duration, if not in perpetuity, for a given quota, which would provide the economic security needed for investment in modern fishing technology. At the same time, and particularly for fishing activities covering different species, whose catches fluctuate at different rates, fishermen must have the necessary latitude to be able to adjust their permit quotas at short notice to match their catches. This constraint argues for the introduction of annual or periodical fishing rights. Taking account of both these types of concern at the same time may lead to two approaches being combined, which is what various countries such as New Zealand, Iceland and the United States have opted to do with regard to fishing (Wallis, 1999).

which are transferable to following years, while setting out in advance the annual quotas allocated to each agent concerned over a long period of time. The permits issued to existing fossil-fired power plants under the *Acid Rain Program*, for example, are valid for a given year but are bankable; in addition, the number of permits that will be assigned to existing plants during the two periods of implementation of the programme (up to 2000; after 2000) have been determined from the outset for the next thirty years.

In the real estate sector, the right to build is linked to the property right to undeveloped land, but irreversibly lost once it is exercised in order to build; there can therefore be no question of renewing such a right annually.

Conditions under which Transfer Rights may be Exercised

Rules regarding transfer are included in the permit specification. There are several different ways in which spatial flexibility and the economic mechanism can be modulated. The following aspects are worth noting:

- A regime in which all agents can freely take part in transfers versus a regime in which participation is restricted on the basis, for example, of sector, territorial area or economic activity;
- A regime of *a priori* free transfer to approve agents associated with *ex post* verification versus a regime under which each projected transfer requires prior authorisation;
- A regime in which a symmetrical right to make transfers permits all approved participants to acquire or sell permits versus a regime based on restricted and asymmetrical transferability; for example, in some programmes, existing facilities are only allowed to sell permits, not to buy them; while new facilities have a monopoly on the purchase of permits.
- As already said, permits to be transferred may be defined in absolute (quotas) or relative (shares) terms. Accordingly, combining user rights and transfer rights options gives way to three main solutions (Table 2). With quotas, user rights and transfers are defined in absolute terms (i.e. tons of CO_2). With credits, user rights are generally defined in relative terms, but transferred credits are defined in absolute terms. With shares, both user rights and permits transferred are defined as shares of an overall ceiling.

With shares systems, absolute amounts cannot be determined *ex ante*. Transactions are therefore subject to some level of uncertainty regarding the reality of rights and requires the agents concerned to carry out calculations which take account of several scenarios, each of which will be assigned a coefficient of probability. This is by no means unusual; many assets in the modern economy are dealt with in this way, one example being shares which shareholders trade on the stock exchanges and which are rights to shares in the capital of quoted companies.

Legal Status of Permits

The economic theory of markets for rights usually regards TPs as property rights held by economic agents. To perform their function (i.e. achieve reductions in costs by allowing transfers), TPs do need to have some characteristics of the ownership of private goods.

Exclusive use is clearly one such characteristic. If TPs allocated to one agent were at the same time allocated to others, or others could legitimately obtain the permits held by the first agent, there would be no sense in trading permits and the mechanism would make no effective contribution to reducing costs. Rivalry among economic agents for access to permits is another such characteristic. If there were no rivalry, each agent could have access to as many permits as he required; it is hard to see how the environment could be protected on that basis. Last, trading means that holders are entitled to transfer their rights to other agents, even if certain schemes only allow intra-firm transactions.

Table 2. **Combinations of User Rights and Transfer Rights Options**

	Transfers of rights defined in absolute terms	Transfers of rights defined in relative terms
User rights defined in absolute terms	(I) Quotas (a, a)	
User rights defined in relative terms	(II) Credits (r, a) (r X i_j = a)	(III) Shares (r, r) (r X q = a)

with a: absolute; r: relative; q: overall quota; i_j: activity index of agent j

Rival demands, exclusive use and the right to transfer are three essential components of full exercise of a property right. For TPs to operate properly, permits need to have the main economic characteristics of a property right. However, twenty years' experience and discussion shows this to be a persistent source of legal and political difficulties; at the same time, administrative solutions can be found if there is a political will to look for them.

In most cases, TPs for pollution control are legally considered to be administrative authorisations, whereas a more conventional property rights approach, running the whole gamut from full private ownership to common ownership via combinations of user rights and servitudes, provides the basis for managing natural resources. Long-lasting controversies about property rights on environmental assets call for specific solutions, in line with the legal traditions in individual countries, to overcome the obstacles that the status of administrative authorisations or common ownership may place in the way of the economic operation of TPs, especially when commercial transactions are involved.

Scope of Application

Sectoral Scope

A TP programme is first and foremost a programme of action designed to achieve certain environmental objectives. To this end, on the basis of a scientific analysis of the phenomena involved, certain activities responsible for the emission of pollutants or abstraction of resources are targeted for government action. The first task of the programme put in place must therefore be to identify the activities and agents which are targeted and to which the programme will apply. The first constraint in this respect is clearly the scope of responsibility of the authority promoting the programme. A domestic programme can therefore only apply to firms subject to the national authority, within the context of regional treaties and international agreements such as WTO. Within this general framework, it will also be necessary to specify which activities and which agents will participate in the programme. The latter population usually consists in a sub-set of the programme's target groups, in that it may prove necessary, for a number of reasons, to reserve the programme to specific categories of agents.

To facilitate the organisation of the system or to gain the trust of regulated agents, it might initially be decided to restrict participation to a given sector, such as the power generation sector, which, despite being a major contributor to the problem of concern is not the only sector involved. In view of the potential transaction or monitoring costs that might be incurred, it might also be decided to impose a minimum scale of activity on firms that would qualify to take part in the programme. Participation could also be limited solely to firms in the productive sector, thus excluding services for which local authorities are responsible despite the fact that these services are also a source of water (wastewater discharges, rainwater run-off) and air pollution (smoke emissions and ash residues from household waste incinerators). Such authorities could be excluded on the grounds that their behaviour is not dictated by economic logic but reflects their public service obligation without any desire to seek profit; by establishing a leak-tight barrier, it might also be a means of ensuring the transparency of fair competition between firms in the productive sector; involving external agents such as local authorities in this sector might give rise to hidden subsidies to certain firms established locally.

These exclusions and restrictions present certain risks and also have implications. There are two types of risk involved:

- They may induce unwanted adverse impacts from an environmental or economic standpoint in that firms may modify the size of their facilities in order to either remain below or, as the case may be, exceed the ceilings that have been set; some firms may reduce the scale of activity of the facilities subject to the new programme, or even close them down, in order to increase activity and emissions at locations where environmental requirements are less stringent (*leakage*);

- They may lead to a contraction in the operating basis of the economic mechanisms (contraction in supply or demand for permits), with the added possibility of the emergence of market power and the use of permit holdings as a barrier to new competitors.

Moreover, the measures taken with regard to agents excluded from the TP programme must make use of other instruments (conventional regulations, taxation) that are assumed to be more appropriate. But this situation of coexistence of different instruments being used *a priori* poses three problems:

- The economic efficiency of the distribution of objectives assigned to different segments, if there is no overall economic mechanism to ensure such economic efficiency across segments;
- The fairness of the distributive impacts borne by the different segments of agents exposed to different instruments; for example, what would happen if agents participating in the TP programme were to be given a free allocation of permits whereas excluded agents were taxed on certain inputs that were indirectly responsible for their emissions?
- Possible overlaps or interference between the different instruments with which the same given firm might be confronted.

Spatial Scale of the System and the Issue of the Territorial Breakdown of the Perimeter to which the System Applies

On what spatial scale should a TP programme be organised? While the answer to this question clearly has an ecological dimension, it also has an economic and institutional dimension. The requirements associated with these two dimensions are in most cases diametrically opposed, which means that the choice must be seen as a trade-off between the two.

Ideally, the spatial coverage of the programme should be determined by the spatial dimension of the environmental problem to be resolved. Problems with water pollution would therefore *a priori* require a framework different to the one that would be appropriate for problems arising from long-distance airborne pollution. Drainage basins and rivers are the natural units to be taken into account for the former, while for the latter the boundaries must be set at the level of a region or a continent and therefore might require co-ordination between a number of countries. It is therefore to be expected that TPs will be developed on very different scales ranging from local to international level.

However, the first constraining factor on any attempt to base programmes on ecological features will be the territorial jurisdiction of the authorities launching the programme, i.e. local, regional or national authorities. There is also an economic aspect. The wider the territorial scope of their jurisdiction and the greater the potential number of transfers, the more scope there should be for making gains on the

Box 7. **The Geographical Dimension of Using TPs to Combat Acid Rain**

In the case of applying the Oslo Protocol to combat long-range acid rain pollution in Europe, there are two extreme solutions that are *a priori* possible with regard to the introduction of TPs: adopt the EMEP grid cells, that is to say relatively small territorial units (150 km × 150 km) as the basic areas within which deposition permit transfers may take place; create a single, unified area as in the case of the United States, namely the area covered by the European Union. In fact, there is also an intermediate solution, and a proposal to that effect has been made under which the European area would be divided into 5 areas of differing sensitivity (Cros and Godard, 1998; Godard, 1999). Relaxing the constraint of the certainty of an improvement in the environment at every point within the territory would increase the economic scope for transfers and reduce abatement costs. Such an initial zoning could also evolve over time to move nearer to the ecological grids used to determine critical loads of acid deposition. TPs would thereby have served as an economic instrument for transition over a period of around thirty years in order to facilitate changes at the various sources by giving them control over the timetable for change. The evolution of zoning criteria would have to be made publicly known to economic agents well ahead of time so that they can form expectations regarding the future constraints of the game and draw up their strategies for change accordingly.

economic costs of pollution abatement and for improving the distribution of abstractions of natural resources. However, the larger the area, the greater the chance that transactions may lead to some local concentration of pollution, which in most cases the authorities try to avoid from an environmental standpoint. On the other hand, the smaller the area, the fewer the opportunities there are for transfers, the higher the costs of transactions and the more that the scope for reducing costs becomes erratic and limited.

These considerations highlight the importance not only of the territorial boundaries of the area covered by the programme but also the internal division of the territory within those boundaries. One possible way of avoiding conflict between the ecological and economic criteria mentioned above might be to divide the area covered by a programme into a number of sub-areas that would serve as the basic units for transfer procedures. A good example of this type of solution, which will be discussed in greater detail in Chapter 2, page 39, may be seen in efforts to combat acid rain (see Box 7).

Participants

Three categories of agent are needed to be specified to organise transfers: (a) those receiving permits under an initial allocation procedure, either directly from the administration or through access to an auction procedure; (b) those licensed to take part in transactions (buying and selling of permits); (c) those who are entitled to use permits in order to emit pollutants or abstract resources.

In the simplest configurations, no distinction is made between the three categories and solely end-users are entitled to take part in transactions, which leaves no room for brokers, for example. In more sophisticated versions category (b) may be extended to include intermediaries (brokers), investors or NGOs, or indeed any person who can exercise his ordinary civil rights; such diversification of the types of operators generally acts as a powerful stimulus on the market and as a force for market organisation in that intermediaries play an important part in reducing part of the transaction costs (i.e., searching partners for trade), even if some of the gains attributable to their actions are reabsorbed through their remuneration.

Examples of Restrictions on Participants

It might prove advisable to introduce restrictions on categories (a) (permit holders) and (c) (permit users). This may be consistent with the objectives that are set, either from an economic standpoint (for example to safeguard the activity of some agents by reserving permits for them) or in terms of the environmental aims. The following examples illustrate this point:

- The aim might be to reserve the use of bought permits solely to new entrants in order to encourage the initial recipients of permits to undertake the changes needed to reduced their emissions or abstractions and at the same to ensure that a large volume of permits is available to new entrants;

- A TP system allows a distinction to be made between two issues: (1) determination of a satisfactory, if not optimal, level of pollution or natural resource abstraction for a given period of time; (2) the most efficient distribution of this ceiling among a set of operators. Regardless of whether it is the outcome of a sound economic calculation or a democratic procedure, the overall ceiling may be treated as an intangible parameter that should not be undermined by the organisation of transfers. The authorities may therefore wish to limit transactions solely to firms that need permits because they emit pollution or abstract resources. The reason for this is that allowing non-users to freeze a proportion of the permits would fail to meet a social welfare efficiency criteria: by inducing a too high level of scarcity for permits and a general increase in the market price of permits, they would thereby impose excessively high costs on all users and distort technological choices (see Figure 3). In contrast, if the authorities consider that the ceiling they have set is relatively arbitrary, in view of the uncertainty over the damage function, then allowing different categories of agent to participate may be a means of better targeting willingness to pay and consequently the desired level of reduction;

Figure 3. **Possible Distortion of Optimal Cap when the Permit Market is Open to Non-Users**

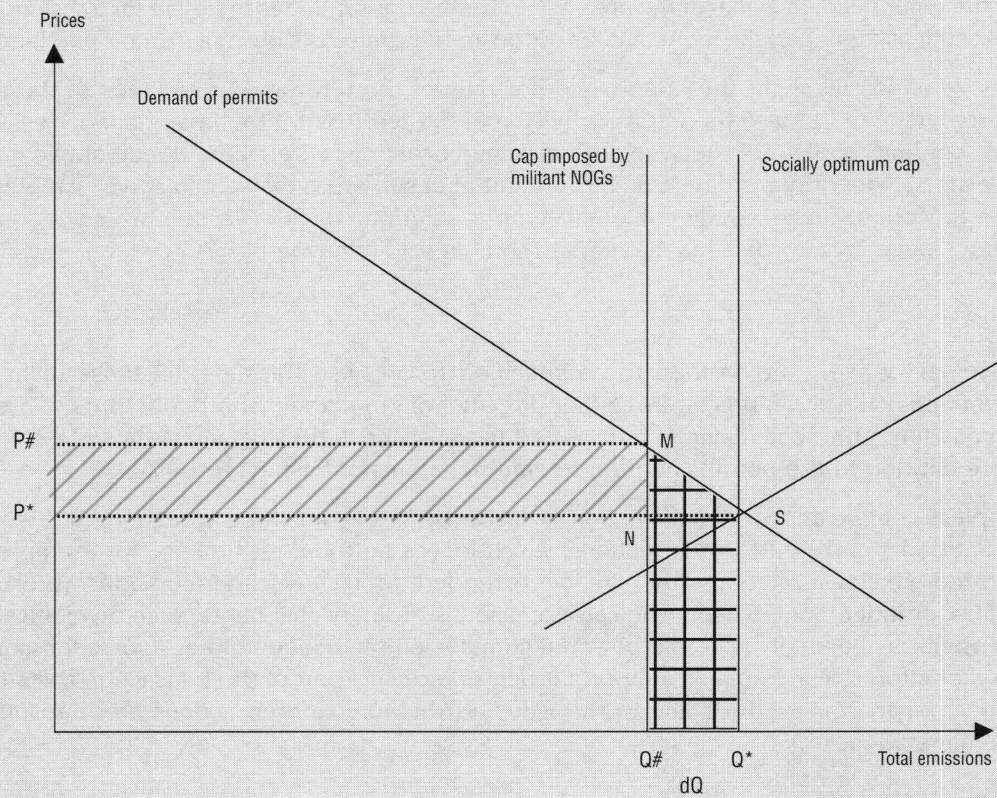

In this figure, by assumption, public authorities have identified the optimal cap on emissions Q*. The decision problem addressed by TPs is the most efficient allocation of this cap between users (firms needing permits to match their emissions). By assumption, militant NGOs place a higher value on environmental protection than society as a whole. If the permit market is open to non-users, NGOs may buy permits aiming at having them frozen. The cap is then switched from Q* to Q#. For this, NGOs have to pay the surface MSQ*Q#. Freezing dQ increases the scarcity of permits for users and, via an increase of the permit price, induce a distortion of choices of polluters who are obliged to use more costly means in order to address the new cap Q#. This imposes on them and society an uncompensated welfare loss equal to the surface P#MNP*. The magnitude of this loss depends on the slope of the social marginal abatement cost curve, reflected in the slope of the demand of permits.

- In systems combining emission permits with deposition permits, only one of the two types of constraint (deposition or emission) represents at any given moment the active constraint on the use of permits by their holder; the surplus permits in the holder's possession might in such cases be considered to be a batch of "non-usable but transferable permits"[3]; they could, however, be purchased by another agent who is not exposed to the same active constraints and who would therefore have the right to use them (Cros and Godard, 1998; Godard, 1999).

Recipients of Initial Permit Allocations

The choice of initial recipients for permit allocations is definitely a decision having a huge distributive dimension. Depending upon circumstances there are two possible strategies:

- Reserve permit allowances to those who are the presumed users in the light of their present or past activity, for example fishing undertakings or fossil-fired power plants; the aim is then to provide the best possible economic conditions for these activities;

- Distribute permits to a large number of agents (for example all the agents participating in fishing activities, such as sailors and dockers, and not simply vessel owners; all the households in a commune concerned by a real estate programme, and not simply landlords; all the adult citizens in a country in the case of permits for emissions of greenhouse gases) in order to distribute the benefits from the rent arising from the programme among the entire community. The end users of permits are thus obliged to buy back permits from all of these recipients in order to pursue their activity. This latter solution has the remarkable property of combining a free issue of permits by the State (no increase in the tax burden) and paying access for those who wish to use a common resource.

Voluntary Participation in the Programme

Contrary to restrictions on participants, it is also possible to authorise the voluntary participation of new entrants such as smaller firms and firms from other sectors responsible for emitting the same pollutants or for abstracting the same resources. This flexible approach to participation can enhance the economic efficiency of the system by increasing the scope for transfers and by improving competition in the transfer market, provided that new entrants are made subject to the same initial constraints as those imposed on mandatory participants.

This option nonetheless carries the risk of introducing a bias into incentives. If the rule for the initial allocation of permits is such that firms can expect to receive an allowance commensurate with their emissions level at the time they join the programme, potential candidates may seek *ex ante* to obtain a scarcity rent either by increasing their emissions or abstractions or by not reducing them by as much as they could. Behaviour of this type was observed in the fishing sector when only a number of fisheries were subject to quota allowances regulated by means of TPs but when it was presumed at the same time that others would subsequently follow suit (Pearse, 1992).

Box 8. **Voluntary Participation in the Acid Rain Program**

The *Acid Rain Program* imposed the mandatory participation of large fossil-fired power plants during the first period of 1995-1999, and was extended to practically all power plants during the next period from 2000 onwards. Those whose participation was mandatory solely during the second period were given the option of voluntarily taking part in the programme during the first period. The same possibilities were offered to industries emitting SO_2, which would ordinarily have continued to remain subject to the conventional regulatory approach but which were given the option of participating voluntarily in the SO_2 TP programme. Since this option entails a change in administrative regime, requiring special monitoring and compliance systems, it cannot readily be reversed.

Design Options for the System

Once a basic framework has been drawn up for the programme (aims, basis, territorial coverage, participants), the next step is to consider in greater detail the variables that will determine the specific direction to give the programme from the standpoint of the organisation of a system of TPs. The following section considers in turn issues relating to the initial allocation of permits, the organisation of different types of flexibility, the organisation of transfers and possible combinations with other instruments such as taxes and voluntary agreements.

Initial Permit Allocation

The procedure for the initial allocation of permits will be substantially different depending upon whether the aim is to introduce a quota system or a programme based on credits or averaging.

Quota Systems

This type of programme consists of setting an overall ceiling or baseline which is then divided into quotas or individual obligations. This section considers the procedures applicable to this stage of permit distribution. This issue is the one which has caused most controversy and conflict. The aim is to find an acceptable rule for a top-down allocation of assets of economic and, more generally, commercial value (fishing rights, abstraction rights, building rights) and, at the same time, for distributing the costly efforts of reducing emissions, or limiting abstraction of natural resources or consumption of the latter among a population of agents. The difficulties associated with this operation are commensurate with the more general difficulty that modern societies find in settling problems relating to the distribution of wealth explicitly and consensually.

Many factors might legitimately be taken into account:

- Possible recognition of moral rights acquired through past practice;
- The desire not to jeopardise the financial viability of agents;
- A similar desire to make the environmental scarcity rent available to the community or at least spreading it very widely among economic agents other than solely those firms emitting pollutants;
- Desire to introduce an equitable and non-arbitrary procedure of allocation;
- Desire to use this stage of initial allocation to create an economic mechanism that will reveal the economic value of permits;
- Introduction of incentives for technical innovation.

Two types of solution are possible: administrative allocation or a market mechanism. The first can be effected on the basis of given criteria, free of charge or at a regulated mandatory price that can be likened to a tax. The second gives free rein to a demand for permits relative to the supply on offer; the price can be free and set through an auction mechanism, or it can be fixed administratively, in which case it loses its economic significance as an index of value.

Criteria for the Free Allocation of Permits to Existing Installations

If the authorities opt for the free allocation of permits, they will then have to decide which criteria should apply to the distribution of permits. However, each actor will demand both a fair set of rules and consideration for his own particular circumstances. This might be contradictory but it is nonetheless by pursuing both these avenues that solutions have been found in practice in those experiments which have proved to be successful (Joskow *et al.*, 1997). On the one hand a basic rule must be drawn up, and on the other the authorities must agree to negotiate around the application of this rule by taking account, at the margin, of certain particular circumstances that may be held to be legitimate.

With regard to the basic rule, it is difficult to determine once for all what an equitable allocation of permits might be, in that there are several different interpretations of what may be deemed to be fair, no one being generally accepted as superseding others:

- Strictly equal distribution, i.e. application of the same "emission quota/value added" ratio to all actors;
- Fairness in terms of the effort made, defined as the share of the cost of pollution abatement in the value added; this criterion is based on the assumption that abatement costs can be known *ex ante* by the supervisory body, which unfortunately is in contradiction with the reasons for which TP systems are usually introduced; another approach, remote from an economic thinking, consists in defining the effort in terms of a percentage reduction;
- "Each according to his needs", which will result in the *pro rata* distribution of emissions resulting from the level of activity that agents envisage achieving over the forthcoming period for which permits will be valid;

- "Each according to his capacity", by taking account of the respective emissions reduction capacity of agents, which would imply that these capacities can be ascertained by the supervisory body without any informational bias;
- "Each in inverse proportion to his contribution to the creation of environmental problems"; in this case those agents who have been the worst polluters over a historical reference period would receive a proportionally smaller quota than the others.

The approach most commonly adopted in practice in based on historical data collected over a given reference period (e.g. averaged over three years) rather than on future projections that are obviously less reliable and that can be manipulated for strategic purposes. This approach corresponds more or less to that of acquired rights, referred to in the United States as "grandfathering". There are several variations to this approach. Depending upon the situation, reference is made to past emissions (a criterion which gives a premium to major emitters who have not yet undertaken to reduce their emissions), the consumption of inputs (energy inputs for instance) multiplied by a standardised emissions coefficient, and market share. Of course it is also possible to use a mix of such criteria. In Australia, for example, the quota for tuna fishing was allocated on the basis of a composite criterion including , with a 25% weight, the value of the vessel and the fishing gear and, with a 75% weight, the average of the best catches over a three-year reference period (Wesney, 1988).

Permit Auctioning Methods

Auctioning consists in the authorities offering permits for money in a procedure placing potential demanders under competition. The auctioning procedure has several advantages. Price formation on the permit market would make it possible to acquire the economic information at the disposal of individual agents and to very rapidly offer an economic benchmark that is common to all actors. Provided that it is organised in an open and transparent manner, the sale of permits would ensure equal access to all the firms placed in competition without introducing a bias into the distribution between the different types of business firms or sectors concerned by the same given programme (e.g. cement plants, steel mills, oil refineries in the case of greenhouse gases) and without making a distinction in the procedures for dividing permits between existing and new installations. Above all, as in the case of taxes, the sale of permits would make it possible to give the instrument a fiscal dimension in addition to its force as an incentive, which could then provide a basis for double-dividend strategies (OECD, 1997; Bureau and Hourcade, 1998).

From a budgetary standpoint, TPs nonetheless exhibit certain disadvantages compared with taxes. With an auctioning procedure, the market sets the price for permits; the tax revenue thereby generated possess an element of unpredictability that the tax authorities do not appreciate, even if they are already accustomed to such unpredictability with regard to other tax bases such as those dependent upon economic activity. Furthermore, in the event that firms might be able to gain access to international permit markets, it is the price of the latter which will determine at what price the authorities within a country can hope selling permits on the domestic market: if firms consider that domestic supply conditions are not advantageous enough, they have the option of procuring permits on the international markets. TPs can therefore perform a fiscal function, although they are undoubtedly more unwieldy than taxes.

Not all auctioning procedures have the same economic properties (Box 9). Some may be unable to fully exploit the potential for trade and may establish a fairly poor balance between supply and demand. For instance, some analyses have been relatively critical of the procedure decided upon by the U.S. EPA and used by the *Chicago Board of Trade* for the annual auction of permits under the *Acid Rain Program* (Cason, 1993). This auction procedure calls for participants to submit sealed bids in which potential vendors specify the number of permits offered for sale and the minimum price asked, and potential buyers the number of permits required and the maximum price they would be prepared to pay. Demand at the highest prices would then be met by supply at the lowest prices until the procedure

Box 9. **Auctioning Techniques**

A distinction may be drawn between sealed-bid and highest-bid auction procedures. In the first type, there are two basic methods for determining payments: (a) the purchaser pays his own price bid at auction; (b) the purchaser pays the auction equilibrium price. These two rules do not produce the same kind of behaviour. In the first case, bidders at the auction attempt to guess the equilibrium price and bid slightly above that price. With the equilibrium price rule, agents who have market power are encouraged to bid below their own price in order to influence the equilibrium price. According to a third rule identified by Vickrey (1961) and applicable to auctions of goods with private value[4], each winner pays the opportunity cost of his victory to the supplier, which means the price that would have been paid by the bidder ranked in second place. This rule cancels out the incentive to make strategic bids and thus the potential market power of certain agents. In the event that the risks of market power are negligible because of the number of agents concerned, the equilibrium price rule is almost as effective as the Vickrey rule (Cramton and Kerr, 1998) but offers several advantages, namely it is simpler, more transparent and leaves more room for manoeuvre for small bidders.

The highest-bid method offers a number of advantages in that it effectively reveals the equilibrium price step by step, which allows bidders to adjust their bids according to actual disclosure of market conditions and not simply on the basis of *a priori* expectations. This is important for goods of common value, as is the case for TPs. With this technique the quantity of permits sought by bidders can only go down, while prices can only go up. At each stage in the process, only the total quantities asked for at a given price are made public. The auction continues until the quantities asked for are slightly lower than the quantities offered. Bidders then pay the price established during the penultimate stage, with a final adjustment being made to the quantities distributed in order to obtain a perfect match with the quantities offered (Cramton and Kerr, 1998).

reached a conclusion at a point deemed to constitute an equilibrium. However, this procedure did not allow supply and demand to be adjusted in accordance with the discovery of information.

If the initial allocation were solely to meet the requirements of economic efficiency and if perfect information on costs were to be available to agents right at the beginning of the programme, this allocation would be efficient from the outset, at least in the short term, and would immediately obviate the utility of permit transfers. The transfer mechanism is therefore designed to offset the inability to achieve a one-shot allocation that is fully efficient in economic terms. It is also designed to take account of the readjustment necessitated by the modification of the main determinants of permit requirements, namely fluctuations in activity due to the economic cycle, technical progress, and enterprise development programmes. The auction procedure therefore does not exclude organisation of a permit market, even though it may make the need for such a market less important.

Auction Procedure for a Partial Share of Quotas

In order to initiate and maintain a permit market once the initial allocation has been made free of charge, it may prove useful to provide for a mandatory auctioning of a limited share of the total quota allowance. Such an auction can play a central role under two sets of circumstances: (1) during the initial introduction of the TP programme when the new routines are not yet in place and most agents still hesitate to commit themselves in trading; (2) if there is no exchange to facilitate transfers and a very wide variety of expectations exists with regard to the value of permits. In both cases the auction procedure helps to rationalise transfers by encouraging the emergence of a reference price that will allow agents to formulate and reach a decision regarding their strategies.

Permits made available through this mechanism may arise from two sources: (a) permits held in reserve by the authorities from the total ceiling set, in which case the income from the sale will go to the public coffers or may be used, through an appropriation account, to finance the cost of operating the exchange and the associated monitoring and compliance services supplied by the administration; (b) a withdrawal on the permits assigned to agents, in which case the income from the sale will ultimately be remitted to the agents concerned; (c) purchases of permits made through transactions between States, in cases where the national permit system is integrated into a larger scheme, as planned for the future prevention of global warming.

Use of Voluntary Agreements

Among the possible solutions which would make it possible to overcome the problems posed by the initial allocation of permits or determination of credits, there is also the option for agents to enter into voluntary agreements negotiated with the authorities. Provided that these agreements are negotiated on a fair basis that is common to all firms, in order to avoid arbitrary discrimination and in order not to jeopardise the principle of equality before the law, they can facilitate acceptance of the sharing of efforts and quotas on the part of those concerned. Associating such agreements with TPs allows the usual inefficiencies of voluntary agreements to be reabsorbed.

Rules of Access for New Entrants

Quota systems pose the specific problem of determining the conditions under which new investors can gain access to permits. Since the total quota has in theory already been divided between existing units, permits needed by new units must primarily be sought on the market, which therefore means that they must be bought. If the initial allocation to existing facilities is made free-of-charge this may act as a brake on the penetration of technical innovation, which often accompanies new investment, and under imperfect competition may also add a new bias into competition. These drawbacks can nonetheless be overcome by various means. For example, the authorities can set up a small reserve of non-distributed permits for sale to new investors at a capped price in order to prevent firms which have benefited from a free initial allocation of permits from holding on to them in order to protect their position.

In contrast, free distribution of permits to new investors is not generally recommended since it would jeopardise compliance with a total ceiling established on the basis of an environmental objective, would undermine the economic rationale for transfers and would be tantamount to sustaining an artificial economic environment in which economic activities do not bear the financial burden of the external environmental costs they impose on society.

Credits

Emission credits constitute a bottom-up rather than a top-down approach to programme organisation. It is not an approach based on the specification of a new environmental objective identified in quantitative terms at a collective level (industrial basin, region, unit area, country). Its general aim is to improve the flexibility and economic efficiency of the general system of standards and regulatory requirements already in place without damaging the environmental performance already achieved. On paper it would seem to be quite straightforward. If firms can prove that their performance in terms of reducing pollution or abstracting resources is actually better than that allowed under the regulations, they can be credited with the additional reduction; once these credits have been certified by an authority, the process of spatial and temporal transfers can begin. In practice, however, this approach faces a number of difficulties.

In many cases the regulations do not specify quantified constraints that are readily measurable and verifiable and include requirements relating to the type of technology or equipment that must be used. As a result it can be difficult to determine the benchmark value for authorised emissions or abstractions. In other words, it may be difficult to translate the regulations in place into quantified emissions or abstraction rights. For the same reasons, it is not uncommon to find that not all emissions from a given source have been duly monitored. For example, it is known that when the *Acid Rain Program* was introduced in the United States in 1995 power plants in that country had to install continuous monitoring equipment to measure their emissions, which shows that until then they did not have a comprehensive system in place to make regular measurements of emissions. Setting a benchmark for acceptable levels of emissions and the ability to measure or estimate emissions reliably are two prerequisites for the introduction of a credit-based approach.

In other cases, the difficulty lies in the fact that at the time when the issue of credit recognition is addressed there may be agents whose performance is already well within regulatory requirements, indeed may have been for some years, which would mean that their current emission levels comfortably meet the standards. There may be two main reasons for this. The first is that improvements in production technology have been introduced, with subsequently lowering of pressure on the environment. The second is the way in which regulatory requirements are framed for activities that fluctuate on various timescales (day, month, year), in that the limit values are calibrated to a plant that is operating at full capacity. However, capacity is generally used at a much lower mean rate, with the result that actual emissions are lower than the level of emissions theoretically authorised. So what should the benchmark value be?

Awarding credits for all the differences which prevail between the current performances achieved in practice at the time that the programme is introduced and the theoretical performances authorised would be tantamount to reintroducing more pollution or resource abstraction into the regulatory system, in that the credits thus authorised could be transferred and used by others. The first effect of the credit-based approach, unless care is exercised, would therefore be to add new pressure on the environment, whereas the aim of the approach is to encourage further reductions! The US approach shows that this is not a theoretical risk (Harrison, 1999). It is not surprising that this credit-based approach has given rise to various objections, which can lead to subsequent disputes, which do not make it any easier to establish clear and transparent rules of the game.

In these various cases, the development of a credit programme first requires the revision of all regulatory requirements in order to supplement them. The first step might therefore be to establish the benchmark on the basis of an average rate of activity based on historical data and not on maximum capacity. A second option would be to base this level on an objective of a future improvement in emissions or abstractions negotiated through voluntary agreements with firms, in which case firms agreeing to a voluntary agreement approach could benefit from a credit-based programme. By definition such agreements would incorporate the concept of a normal reduction in emissions at different future stages and would only acknowledge credits with regard to reductions over and above those objectives. This offers a means of transforming the credit-based approach into an instrument which would undoubtedly improve the environment. However, this solution does not do away with the need for reliable measurements and estimates of total emissions and the activity parameters of a facility at the various time periods taken into account.

Approaches Based on Relative Values and Averaging

Unit-Value Approaches

The absolute value approach (quotas) is, *a priori*, simpler for the public authorities than an approach based on relative values in that it allows a straightforward link to be established to environmental goals expressed in the form of quantities caps and facilitates the organisation of transfers. However, there are a number of reasons why certain actors are more attracted to approaches based on permits expressed in relative values.

Some economic actors whose activity is sensitive to the business cycle or exposed to various contingencies ask for benefiting from TPs defined in relative values and not absolute ones. It may be noted that this method, up to a certain point, is close to that used in major projects such as the *Acid Rain Program* in the United States and the RECLAIM programme in the Los Angeles district (Harrison, 1999; Schwarze and Zapfel, 1999), in which the initial allocation is defined firstly on the basis of a unit emission rate per energy input unit and subsequently multiplied by the quantities of inputs used over a certain period.

The practical implication of a relative value approach is that the emission rights granted to agents vary according to the level of their activity and without the latter having any need to buy additional permits or sell unused ones. When allowed emission levels are defined on the basis of unitary emission rates $\mathbf{T}_n$ and actual emissions are lower at $\mathbf{T}_r$, the credits obtained will depend on the actual level of activity of facility $\mathbf{A}_t$ during period $\boldsymbol{t}$, by a formula of the type $\mathbf{C}_t = (\mathbf{T}_n - \mathbf{T}_r)\mathbf{A}_t$. When firms are expanding their activities, their emission or abstraction rights expand themselves too at no cost for them. However, in this scenario, total emissions will rise, which would represent a potential deterioration in the situation with regard to the environment.

This approach therefore poses the specific problem of integration with policies designed to achieve levels of environmental performance defined in terms of absolute volumes of pollutant emissions. Variations in industrial activity (the business cycle, for instance, meaning changes in capacity utilisation) would result, for the same given relative performance, in changes in number of permits awarded to economic agents and potentially traded. When it is absolutely imperative to meet an overall volume constraint, then changes in emissions from a sector subject to a system defined in relative values would have to be offset by other counter-veiling mechanisms in that sector or elsewhere. If other sectors were to be exposed to fluctuations in the requirements to which they themselves are subject, then the comfort and economic security of some firms would be achieved at the cost of the economic insecurity of others (see Chapter 2, page 27 and Box 5).

Despite these disadvantages, this approach might nonetheless be of practical interest with regard to one aspect of regulating the permit system, which is as follows. One traditionally thorny problem in the design of TP programmes is how to deal with the closure of production facilities which hold a number of permits. Should they lose their permits or should they be allowed to redeem the permits that the closure has saved? In addition to which there is concern in some local communities but also at regional or national levels that giving firms the option of redeeming permits by closing their facilities might simply amount to an additional financial incentive for them to relocate their activities to other regions or countries. If the permits allocated are defined in relative values, then the number of permits decreases in proportion to the decrease in the level of activity of plant and are no longer valid in the event of closure. There is therefore no additional incentive for firms to relocate. In terms of the political acceptability of permits, this advantage might outweigh the additional uncertainty arising over the absolute level of emissions from agents subject to relative value permits, at least with regard to those firms for which the risk of opportunistic relocation is the greatest.

Averaging

Averaging is aimed at the regulatory specifications regarding manufactured goods whose use involves the consumption of energy and generation of various types of polluting emissions. These specifications are formulated in unit values such as consumption of fuel per kilometre travelled or the hydrocarbon density of discharges to the atmosphere.

The implicit allocation of permits therefore depends upon three factors: the required improvement in the technical performance of a class of products (percentage reduction); the estimated initial value, at a given reference date, for the various models or sub-categories in a range of products in the same given product class; forecast of the respective volume of sales and utilisation of the various models. It is then possible to establish a link between the formulation of an average performance standard and its quantified impact on the overall volume of emissions. Here, unlike in the previous case, the credits approach can be made compatible with compliance with an overall cap or baseline set by the authorities; for instance the benchmark for crediting can be defined by the product of unit limit values and the level of output at the reference year; subsequent increases in production should then be more than offset by increases in efficiency of products put on the market for giving birth to credits.

Organisation of Temporal and Spatial Flexibility

There are a number of ways in which flexibility can be introduced into programmes in order to tailor them to a specific problem or objective. Such flexibility may be in either temporal or spatial terms, although in practice some instruments are flexible in both respects.

Forms of Temporal Flexibility

These types of organisation allow TPs valid for one period to be transferred to another period. They have the great advantage of allowing agents to optimise their strategies for managing environmental problems over time, even though it is primarily in the case of cumulative problems that the greatest advantage is to be gained, whereas the margins on temporal flexibility are far narrower in the case of problems where the damage to the environment depends more on flows than on stocks. In the case of fisheries management, for example, where the dynamics of interacting living populations have to be addressed, flexibility over time would raise special problems in monitoring and co-ordinating the time strategies of each agent to ensure that, within each period, fishing catches are compatible with sustainable exploitation of resources. In themselves means of temporal flexibility do not require any transaction between separate economic agents, but they do not rule them out either. By offering an alternative, they can therefore compete with external market transactions.

Budgets Valid for a Given Period

The period may be for a period of three months, a year or several years (5 or 10). The choice of the duration of the period must take account of the nature of the problems targeted but also the conditions under which a credible assessment can be made of the performances achieved, given that long-term periods can undermine the credibility of the programme by extending the deadline for verification of compliance with the new constraints.

To ensure the liquidity of transfers and avoid transfers peaking at the term of each period, it might be advisable to divide the agents participating in the programme into two groups of equal size whose compliance periods overlap, with the periods of the one group ending in the middle of the period of the other group. This is the solution adopted by the RECLAIM programme (Harrison, 1999).

Banking

With banking, a firm does not forfeit the unutilised portion of emission permits valid for a given period; it can employ them over one or more subsequent periods. The consequences for the environment and for costs both have to be gauged.

From the environmental standpoint, this approach is acceptable only when the type of pollution involved is damaging on account of the stock of pollutants accumulated over successive periods, not the flows emitted in one given period, or when banking is part of a programme of major reductions, stage by stage, in authorised emissions. In the former case, transfers from one period to another are neutral in terms of the environment. In the latter case, exceeding the objectives set by the authorities in terms of emissions reductions at early stages can yield both environmental and economic benefits, as explained thereafter.

When the marginal damage to the environment is a rising function of the level of emissions, the transfer of permits from a period when pollution is still high and excessive to another during which such pollution will have been significantly reduced due to changes in ceilings or regulatory constraints will result in an overall environmental gain due to the lower level of damage over the sum of the two periods concerned: early overcompliance is generally good for the environment and people's health. There are situations in which the environmental benefit of banking is significantly higher than the savings in abatement costs achieved by firms. This would appear to be the case in the provisions made for permit banking in the averaging programme that was applied to car exhaust emissions in California (Rubin, 1993).

From an economic standpoint, transferring permits that have been banked allows firms to alleviate the far more severe constraint that will be imposed in following stages. Depending upon individual circumstances, firms may be able to achieve significant gains in terms of pollution abatement costs. Besides the discounting rate, this will depend, in fact, on the slope of the curve representing the marginal pollution abatement cost and the respective values of the rate of decrease in the number of emission permits issued and the rate of technical progress with regard to the options available for reducing emissions. If the rate of technical progress is higher than the decrease of allowed emissions, abatement costs could decline over time despite the increased stringency of the constraint and then banking could not be profitable at all for agents. However, unless there are some unforeseen innovations, this theoretical possibility of a decline in marginal costs is scarcely plausible in practice since policy-makers usually take account of the prospects for technical progress when setting pollution abatement targets.

Above and beyond the *ex post* cost-benefits of transfers between different time periods, the temporal flexibility afforded by banking gives economic agents scope to introduce smoothed abatements in successive stages, thus allowing them to lessen the impact of sharp changes in ceilings from one stage to another (see Figure 4) or, on the contrary, to invest at a particular point in time in order to be able to achieve a highly significant reduction in emissions over several subsequent periods. Banking also allows firms to ensure that they have a sufficient reserve of permits to meet their anticipated needs so that they can continue to operate their facilities. Compared with a strategy based on the possibility of making external permit transactions in the future to meet anticipated needs, the option of banking permits is all the more attractive to regulated agents in that their perception of future market conditions is affected by uncertainty and unpredictability to some extent. This would not be quite so much the case if forward transactions were readily available.

On the other hand, when harm to health or the environment depends on the flow of pollutants or abstractions over a fairly short reference period (a day, a month, a year), banking would mean that pollution or abstraction could well be unacceptably concentrated during a critical period. For this reason the method cannot be employed in all cases. It is in fact suitable for cumulative problems or ones involving diffuse long-distance phenomena, or else in programmes to preserve natural resources and environmental quality in areas where quality is good. But it is not suitable for local pollution affecting people's health in areas failing to meet environmental standards in spite of the early gains for health derived from overcompliance in the initial periods. For example the RECLAIM programme of TPs for SO_2 and NO_x in Los Angeles, focusing on local pollution, does not allow banking.

Figure 4. **Smoothing Emission Reductions Subject to Ceilings P1, P2 and P3 over Several Periods**

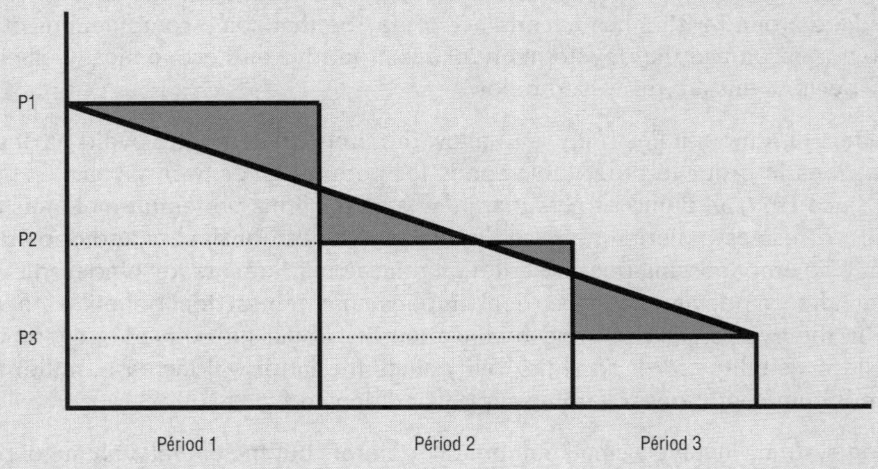

Stricter ceilings, P1, P2 and P3 are phased in over three periods, resulting in step increases in the constraint. Anticipating an appreciable increase in costs during the following two periods, an agent makes early reductions (at lower cost) in period 1 (the shaded triangle under the cap), enabling him to increase his emissions in period 2 and 3 (shaded triangles over caps) in relation to the ceiling for that period. He thereby optimises his use of TPs available for the three periods, and in particular smoothes his reduction efforts as illustrated below.

There is a halfway house between allowing banking without any time limitation, and not allowing it at all. In this approach, permits held back for later use are whittled down, or discounted: a permit allowing emissions of 100 in period 1 will give entitlement to emissions of 90 in period 2, and 70 in period 3, and so on, or else banking will be permissible for a few periods only, three for instance, so as to lessen the concentration of emissions or abstractions over time.

Borrowing

Borrowing provides flexibility over time similar to that provided by banking. Like banking, there may be an economic interest, allowing firms to adjust their reduction schedule to their investment programmes to modernise plant or extend capacity, and to their scope to incorporate technical advances. It also assists adjustments made necessary by the business cycle or changes in circumstances, such as weather, which influence the degree of economic activity of some emission or abstraction sources.

It has to be said that this method raises many fundamental reservations about the political economy of public choice on environmental matters. It allows economic agents to postpone action that other parties would prefer to see launched as quickly as possible. It is hard to argue that this course provides any environmental advantage, except very hypothetically and indirectly through the cost savings to economic agents: the savings might make the introduction of stiffer environmental targets over the medium and longer term more acceptable to agents.

Borrowing in fact gives rise to two main concerns. The first is that firms may launch into an endless spiral of borrowing against future rights and thus, for many years, evade reducing their current levels of emission or abstraction. The second is that, after using up their scope for borrowing, firms may tell the authorities that they are simply unable to comply with the initial objectives, and renegotiate environmental constraints to their advantage[5].

Linkages Between Temporal and Spatial Flexibility

It is not possible to assess the merits of the various options for temporal flexibility without considering how they could be combined in economic terms with opportunities for external transfers between separate agents. The question is this: are they complementary, or relatively incompatible? Generally speaking, once there are clear and credible rules of the game, an economist will emphasise the advantages of greater flexibility since it enables agents to select the strategies which are best for them. But in a world where transaction costs are significant and in the introductory stage of a new instrument, hedged around with much uncertainty, it may be that some combinations of the two types of flexibility do not encourage the development of a competitive and economically efficient market for permits. Two aspects of this are discussed below.

The first effect of temporal flexibility is to allow the firms concerned to avoid having to undertake external transactions in order to meet their needs for permits. Over twenty years' experience in the United States, since 1977, all demonstrates that in most cases firms prefer internal transfers to external ones (see Box 10). This easy solution necessarily weakens the establishment and operation of a permit market. This may be embarrassing because external transactions are already hindered by informational asymmetry that affects pricing – a good deal implies that transaction benefits are divided in an equitable way in the eyes of agents – and by uncertainties about future market conditions, which are increased by the possibility of temporal flexibility since the latter will increase, rather than diminish, uncertainty over future conditions regarding supply and demand.

Lastly, when systems involve a small number of operators but the overall volume of permits is high, temporal flexibility may allow some agents to secure market power. But if the rules ban any temporal flexibility permits lose all practical and monetary value as each period elapses, holders of unused permits for that period will have an incentive to put them on the market before they lose their value, thus raising the supply; at the same time they are unable to accumulate a mass of permits which would give them strategic influence over the market.

Box 10. **The Preference for Internal Transfers as Shown by the US Experience**

Over nearly five years of reported transactions (March 1994-December 1998) under the Acid Rain Program, more than 60% of transfers were internal ones. Out of the 8.7 million SO_2 emission permits allocated in 1995, 4.76 million were used by their holders, 0.53 million were sold to other agents for use in 1995 and 3.4 million were banked for a year or a subsequent period either internally or following external transactions (Ellerman *et al.*, 1997, pp. 34-35). In fact, between 25 and 50% of permits allocated during phase 1 of the programme (1995-1999) are thought to have been banked for use in phase 2 (2000 onwards), when emission constraints will be twice as strict (Bohi *et al.*, 1997).

The American programme for *lead-free petrol* is a good example of the points discussed in this section: rights to add lead were widely traded among refineries, appreciably lowering the costs of adjusting refining plant (Nussbaum, 1992; Howe, 1994). This success is attributable to a number of factors, of which two may be noted here. To begin with, the programme covered a limited number of years, so there was no prospect of strategic use of banking; accordingly, firms were better off making external transactions. In addition, dealings in lead permits developed from an established practice of regular trading in a number of products among refineries, and lead permits were simply an extra item in this process. The circumstances are somewhat exceptional; as a rule, holders of emission permits have no standing practice of trading a range of products between them. That highlights the important role of intermediaries (brokers) to facilitate dealings, meaning that the volume of external transactions needs to be high enough for them to become involved.

To conclude, while temporal flexibility may have an economically important role to play, especially when opportunities for external transactions are few, it can also inhibit the development of an external competitive permit market. At the same time, banking encourages early reductions in emissions, from the outset of a programme of TPs, at a time when the market is not properly established. So a number of considerations are involved here, and it is not easy to strike the right balance.

Systems Affording Spatial Flexibility

These methods allow spatial transfers of permits to emit pollutants, to abstract natural resources (water, fish) or to build (land-use permits). These transfers may or may not entail transfers of rights between separate economic agents. Over some ten years (1977-1986) in the United States, for instance, only 10% of transfers under the offset programme involved separate economic agents, the others being internal transactions within a firm owning several facilities (Hahn and Hester, 1989*a* and *b*).

In theory, free transfer of permits should be encouraged because of a clear advantage in terms of costs, provided that transfers are neutral from the standpoint of residual environmental damage. That is not necessarily the case. From the environmental standpoint, the main problem with spatial transfer systems lies in assessing acceptable equivalence between damage caused by emissions or abstractions at different places in the area. Differences in the location of emissions or abstractions will entail differences in location of deposits or physical impact and, potentially, differences in environmental damage.

There are two reasons for this: (1) the recipient environments are not the same, and do not have the same sensitivity to pollution deposits or abstractions; (2) one deposit point or one downstream ecosystem may receive deposits from a number of sources or feel the cumulative effects of a number of abstractions, thus generating localised concentrations of risk exposure; usually the ecological damage or pollution function is not linear in relation to deposits and levels of environmental pressure, and concentrations generate high damage locally, which may be judged unacceptable.

From the economic and social standpoint, the differences in environmental damage associated with spatial transfers also have a distributive dimension depending on the geographical spread of population groups (urban areas, rural areas) and income categories. Even if the environmental damage is the same in objective terms, spatial transfers have it borne by different people, which may not be disregarded.

Although some experts now tend to think that problems arising from the concentration of pollutants at certain locations have been overestimated in the past, it is useful to outline some of the strategies that might be adopted towards this problem.

Ecologically Neutral Emission Bubbles

The first approach consists in dividing the geographical area covered by the programme into a series of bubbles whose boundaries are designed to ensure that the level of ecological damage from pollutant emissions and abstractions is equivalent at all points within one same bubble. In practical terms the criterion used is quite straightforward, i.e. the point at which emissions or abstractions take place within each bubble must be considered irrelevant. In contrast, transactions between one bubble and another are not allowed.

Bubbles in an Ecologically-Heterogeneous Context

The second approach moves away from the concept of environmental damage equivalence. It allows trading of permits in circumstances where it cannot be postulated that environmental damage will be equivalent. The risk involved is counter-balanced by imposing a stringent programme to reduce total emissions or resource abstractions over a given area. Although sources are free to transfer permits, there is accordingly a strong presumption that environmental conditions will improve right across the area. In formal terms, this approach looks very much like the earlier one. It is the one adopted by the United States for the Acid Rain Program, in spite of protests by individual states which were apprehensive that scope to transfer emissions would lead to a deterioration in quality in particularly sensitive and valued areas (nature reserves)[6].

Deposition Bubbles

The third approach is based on the concept of a "deposition bubble". Since the only direct action that firms can take to control the deposition of the pollutants they emit is on their emissions, with this approach the programme must be based on a reliable model of pollutant dispersion modes or impact chains. The aim is therefore to establish a function which determines the quantity deposited depending on the quantity emitted, for each source and each target point.

In the case of atmospheric pollution, however, dispersion is dependent on meteorological conditions and statistical determination is not fully reliable. This may well create legal uncertainties for firms; for a given emission flow, the only variable over which they have direct control, the effect in terms of deposits at target points will be uncertain, and unknown in advance. To minimise the consequences of this, they would need a simple procedure for settling balances at regular intervals and a very fluid permit market, which seems rather unlikely in a system with as many separate markets as there are target points and where a major problem of separability arises: deposits from a given source at different target points are related via the emission flow from which they come, meaning that agents cannot manage their various pollutant deposits separately. To make the position of firms legally more secure, permits assigned to sources would then have to be defined as emission or abstraction permits via a standardised conversion of deposit permits or impact indicators.

Given the operational complications involved, this approach has not so far been put into practice.

Offset Systems

With an offset system, transfers between different bubbles are authorised on the basis of exchange coefficients designed to take account of the differences in damage that may result from transfers (Amann *et al.*, 1994). When we have N basic areas (N bubbles), this approach means defining $(N^2 - N)/2$ coefficients. For these coefficients to be perfectly valid in economic terms, it would be necessary to establish that the marginal damage associated with the emission of additional units of pollutant in zone *i* is equal, in proportion to the coefficients, to the marginal damage arising from the emission of an additional unit of pollutant in zone *j*. This approach is hardly feasible and must therefore be replaced by other, less perfect ones, given that, in order to provide an accurate indication of marginal damage over time, the value of coefficients would have to be revised after each transaction, which is obviously not feasible in practical terms. It is for this reason that Bailey, Gough and Millock (1994) proposed using coefficients for the physical transfer of pollutants from sources to recipients, weighted by the assumed scale of damage incurred in the recipient zone. The exchange rate between two sources is then the ratio of the two transfer coefficients:

$$\text{Exchange rate}_{1,2} = \frac{\sum_k \left(T_{1,k} \cdot G_k\right)}{\sum_k \left(T_{2,k} \cdot G_k\right)}$$

where $T_{i,k}$ = transfer coefficient from i to k and
G_k = scale of damage for a deposit above the critical threshold in zone k

If the offsetting approach is adopted, it may be advisable to apply to the latter a procedure that is separate to the one applicable to transfers within each bubble, i.e. to provide for a prior authorisations regime based on a simulation of the potential impacts of the projected transfers in order to verify that there is no concentration of pollution. An *ad hoc* modelling tool should be used for this purpose, in accordance with the approach that has already been adopted by the UN Economic Commission for Europe in charge of the Convention on Long-Range Airborne Pollution.

Box 11. **The US System of Offsets**

The system of offsets established in the United States is based on a fairly similar approach to the one we have just examined: the country is divided into 247 areas, classified as attainment areas and non-attainment areas depending on whether or not they comply with federal air quality standards. When a new facility is to be set up in a non-attainment area it has to obtain emission permits from existing sources in a proportion determined by the offset rate applying to the particular area. Set by the administration, offset rates reflect the degree to which ambient air standards are currently exceeded. The 1990 Clean Air Act Amendments stiffen offset rates for tropospheric ozone, by establishing five categories with five offset rates: 1.10; 1.15; 1.20; 1.30; 1.50. But the selection of these rates is not directly tied to comparative assessment of the marginal damage associated with pollution.

Organisation of Transfers

Transfers can take a variety of forms. If they take place within the same firm, they may not necessarily be commercial transactions. Outside the firm, they may take the form of bilateral commercial transactions, trades in an exchange pool, transactions organised by a broker or other intermediaries, or transfers carried out under the auspices of an administrative authority, for example as part of a programme of industrial rationalisation; in the latter case, compensation may take the form of a lump-sum payment or in some cases transfers may not have any readily identifiable counterpart. Transfer contracts may be drawn up with immediate effect or may only enter into force after a certain period of time. They may be firm contracts, whose conditions have all been drawn up in advance, or simply contingent contracts in which some variables such as the transfer price will depend upon certain events taking place in the future under conditions specified beforehand. They may also consist of options. For example, the purchaser may secure an option to carry out the agreed transfer at a given date, in which case the vendor is obliged to comply, but conserves the opposite option not to carry out the transfer, to which the vendor gives his agreement in advance. Transfers can also be carried out directly on the initiative and under the control of the partners themselves, or may require a procedure for prior administrative authorisation to provide various guarantees. All these forms of transfer do not have the same economic features and do not provide the same benefits.

It might be helpful at this point to review some of the more important points.

The Role Played by Permit Exchanges

Permit exchanges can play a useful role in ensuring the efficient organisation of transfers either as a supplement to bilateral transactions or, in some specific circumstances, as an institution with a monopoly on the organisation of transactions.

Being able to create a competitive market through an exchange offers a number of significant advantages. It avoids some of the pitfalls of bilateral transfers when transfers must take place against a background of highly imperfect and asymmetrical information. It makes it possible to attenuate the risks of market power and allows all regulated agents equitable access to the benefits of permit transfers. It generates a public price, which is an essential feature of the operation of a decentralised economy.

In most cases, making provision for several forms of transfer is the best way of ensuring that the market will work properly. This is not always the case, however. If there is a risk that the number of external transfers will remain low due to the transaction costs and if the authorities consider this situation to be a source of significant economic inefficiencies, it may be advisable to seek to centralise transfers within an institutionalised exchange. The idea of granting a monopoly to an exchange institution was the solution adopted by Iceland in 1998 with regard to fishing. All external trading in fishing quotas must now take place within a single exchange which the Icelandic Parliament voted to set up for this purpose (Wallis, 1999). In addition to which, provisions could be made whereby trades can only be made during specific periods and would be banned the rest of the time. This restrictive approach would be aimed solely at concentrating supply and demand within the exchange in order to generate transfer flows above the minimum volume required to establish a competitive market. This period of time could be a week, month, quarter or year depending upon the nature of the situations to be regulated.

Market for Immediate Delivery and Futures Markets

As with all other shares and assets, TPs can *a priori* be traded in transactions with immediate or delayed effect. By determining prices and volumes *ex ante*, forward transactions have the major advantage of offering different securities to agents who wish to preserve good operating conditions for their plant or meet in advance the conditions for new projects. This also allows these agents to protect themselves against the possible use of market power in the future. Naturally, by authorising speculative transfers, forward transactions and options markets also generate a systemic risk which may have a feedback effect on the operation of the market, as in other markets of this type.

Box 12. **Forward Transactions in the Acid Rain Program**

The electricity utilities can agree to any forward transfers of permits on the sole obligation that they register them at the point in time when one of the partners intends to use the permits to cover his emissions. Provided that these utilities know what their future endowment of annual allowances will be over a period of thirty years, it is possible that forward transactions have already taken place, even though they have still not yet been accounted for in the tracking system of the Federal Environmental Protection Agency. On the other hand, the annual auctioning procedure organised under the auspices of this agency offers two types of market: a market for permits with immediate effect and a future market for permits to be used several years ahead.

This approach is not really appropriate to credit systems in that the credits that will be validated will generally only be determined *ex post* after a given period of time. Agents therefore do not know in advance how many credits they will have and forward transactions become a risky business.

A distinction must carefully be drawn between forward transactions and systems designed to allow flexibility over time, as discussed above, which allow to transfer permits from one period to another. Forward transfers in themselves do not change the period during which a permit may be used. For example, an agent might sign in 1999 a contract for the acquisition in 2005 of a permit that will enter into force in 2008, while borrowing would mean that an agent will use in 2005 a permit valid for 2008.

Bilateral Transfers Based on Transport and Pollutant Flow Impact Models

The desire to ensure that the transfer system remains flexible argues in favour of keeping administrative procedures simple and in particular of avoiding the use of prior authorisations whenever possible with regard to environmental quality objectives. The literature nonetheless contains proposals that seek to facilitate bilateral transfers by basing them on a centralised model for the transport and impact of pollutant flows. These proposals concern situations in which the recipient environments are different and in which transfers modify the environmental impacts. In such cases modelling is expected to identify beforehand those transfers which would reduce costs and improve environmental quality in each unit area. The mechanism therefore combines a physical model for pollutant dispersal and an economic model based on the cost of abating emissions in different bubbles.

In the situations considered, the order in which transfers are made has a major impact on the equilibrium of distribution that can be reached and also the ability to achieve an economically efficient distribution: after each transfer has been completed, the scope for new transfers is modified and the interplay between discontinuities can lock the distribution of permits into a sub-optimal configuration.

It is for this reason that Van Ierland, Kruitwagen and Hendrix (1994) proposed the introduction of what they termed a "guided bilateral exchange" to implement the Oslo protocol on acid rain. The comparison of emissions arising from allocations between countries, as determined under the protocol, and the optimum allocation calculated by means of the model would determine the total set of potential trades that would amount to a gain in economic efficiency. When a proposed bilateral trade examined by the supervisory authority is part of this set, it is approved; if it is not, then it is turned down. It is only when all desirable bilateral transactions have been completed that an economically efficient allocation will have been achieved through this procedure.

The validity of this centralised model approach towards transfers depends upon the quality of the physical, ecological and economic data input to the model. There is a certain internal contradiction that might perhaps be detected in this approach in that the introduction of TPs is usually justified as an answer to the central authorities' lack of information; if the authorities were able to centralise the information needed to draw up a reliable and optimal plan for reducing emissions, why would they still want to give decentralised agents the freedom and responsibility to carry out transfers on their own initiative?

Combination with Other Instruments

Transferable Permits and Taxes

In situations of uncertainty about cost and damage functions, when the authorities want both to have certain guarantees of improved physical performance and to avoid exposing agents to economic costs deemed to be excessive, it may be advisable to combine a TP system with taxation applicable to the same regulated population.

One possible way of doing this, based on an initial proposal by Roberts and Spence (1976), is as follows. On the one hand, in order to be reasonably confident of achieving a given level of environmental performance, the authorities could set a quantified emissions constraint which would then serve as a basis for issuing TPs to agents. On the other hand, in order to place a cap on the maximum unit costs of compliance with this constraint, a full-discharge tax would be introduced to allow agents who might have to bear costs deemed to be excessively high to overshoot their TP allowances. The level of this tax would have to be set as representing the estimated maximum unit cost the competent authority considers it reasonable to charge in order to obtain a decrease in emissions. This level would theoretically be higher than the average expectations concerning the market value of permits. A tax of this type should not be confused with a penalty or sanction designed to prevent or punish a reprehensible act. A bottom rate would also be set for permits at which the authorities would be entitled to tighten the constraint by buying back permits from their holders. Thus if the authorities observed that the market price was unexpectedly low, this would be that the basis they had used to calculate the emissions constraint was erroneous, which would justify an *ex post* revision. In the same vein, a tax approach could be applied not to the entire physical basis chosen (emissions, energy inputs, abstractions) but on upper part of it, which comes to allow quotas for free for the other part. In that case, the untaxed quota could be made transferable.

Further, a small tax on permits hold by the regulated agents, to avoid strategic retention of permits and induce holders to sell unused entitlements, could also be introduced. As any tax on asset ownership, it could help in the creation of a well-functioning market and facilitate an efficient allocation of permits among participants.

Another way of combining taxes and TPs is to use TPs only for some groups of agents and taxes for the others. This differentiated treatment can be justified by transaction, monitoring and enforcement costs that can be excessively high if permits were used by some groups of agents (for instance car owners). Care should be given to deliver coherent economic signals through different instruments. The distributive consequences of a joint use of TPs and taxes should also be considered. For instance, taxing final consumers and granting a free allocation of TPs to business firms is tantamount to organising an income transfer from consumers to shareholders since the former will have to pay taxes plus price increase on the market for goods related to the environmental programme imposed on firms, while the latter pay no tax and can benefit the scarcity rent generated by the environmental programme. Such a transfer of income may or may not be defensible on political or equity ground. Anyway, it may be advisable to define the physical basis of both instruments in the same way, in order to facilitate comparisons at the border of the two systems.

Transferable Permits and Voluntary Agreements

Efforts might be made to foster synergies between TPs and voluntary agreements. In recent years both government and industry in several countries have expressed an interest in voluntary, negotiated approaches, primarily because they allow a policy to be put in place more rapidly and on a more consensual basis than with instruments requiring changes in legislation. In this respect, linking TPs to voluntary agreements would offer the major advantage of eliminating the problems with implementation failures and the economic inefficiencies usually associated with voluntary agreements when the latter are not accompanied by other legal and economic mechanisms. However a condition has to be met, that a regulatory framework should be already in place in order to allow administrative services or an agency to take initiatives in organising TPs.

In a scenario of this kind, a company can obtain transferable credits if its performance is better than that required by the agreement; on the other hand, if its performance falls short of the requirement it has to make up the shortfall by purchasing permits. This solves the problem of sanctions for failure to meet performance objectives, at least in respect of commitments denominated in homogeneous quantities, as in the case of gas emissions. There are two more general constraints that must be met here, however. Firstly the voluntary agreements must relate to homogeneous target variables that could subsequently be incorporated into a TP system. Secondly, voluntarily agreed targets must be monitored and enforced by public authorities with the same vigour as standard TP schemes. Rules specifying environmental requirements and rights would in any case have to be provided for agents not wishing or unable to enter into such voluntary agreements.

Means of Application

Once the basic framework and the principal variables characterising the type of TP system considered have been chosen, the next step is to provide the elements that will allow it to work in practice. These elements include (a) a system to monitor pollutant emissions and resource abstraction; (b) means to encourage agents to comply strictly with requirements and not to exceed the emission or abstraction levels for which they hold permits; and (c) means to promote participation by agents and to ensure that the programme is run smoothly and fairly.

Means of Information

The ability of agents and the administrative authority to have access to reliable and precise information over time, provided by the characteristic variables used to define constraints, is a prerequisite for the successful operation of a TP scheme. In some respects, it would be fair to say that TPs primarily consist of infrastructure for monitoring and recording emissions, rights and transfers. At least three types of operation therefore have to be envisaged:

- Systems of direct monitoring of emission and abstraction data or collection of indirect information about such performance have to be organised, responsibility being assigned either to permit users (self-policing) or to third parties; this often entails installing new measuring devices at the sources covered by the programme;
- Information on performance and transfers made has to be sent in an appropriate form (format, frequency) to a supervisory authority or policing body.
- Accounts of actual performance and permit allotment have to be kept and periodically updated; it is of vital importance that the information contained in these accounts be placed in the public domain in order to ensure that the programme has credibility in the eyes of both participants and the general public.

Naturally the measurements and information collected must relate directly and unambiguously to the phenomenon addressed by the programme, particularly at the stage when the frequency of measurements needs to be determined.

Entrusting responsibility for these operations to agents, on the basis of self-assessments and binding declarations, in most cases allows information to be gathered at the closest point to the phenomena concerned, or at least for emissions or abstraction related issues. It also allows public agencies to reduce their costs. But the performance of these operations by agents themselves must not give rise to biases that might jeopardise data reliability and objectivity. Meeting this requirement usually requires precise regulations regarding the type of measurement system permissible or procedures for the collection and processing of information, as well as verification. The latter may be carried out directly by the administration or ensured through the requirement that agents be certified by independent certification companies. Third party involvement is not a solution for managing systems based on pollutant deposition or compliance with ambient quality standards, which call for other kinds of collective organisation such as measurement networks managed in partnerships by the actors concerned.

An alternative arrangement would be to base information on different types of sensor and meter placed under the direct operational control of a supervisory agency. The responsibility for managing the investment and maintaining the monitoring system would therefore be transferred to this agency and, where necessary, to the public authorities.

In view of the cost of direct measurement systems, such as those requiring emissions sensors to be installed at all source locations, it is advisable to systematically determine whether other solutions that would yield similar information, of sufficiently high quality but at cheaper cost, were available. Under the Acid Rain Program, the continuous monitoring of emission sources was made mandatory for various gases, but in the case of CO_2, an assessment-based approach was accepted in which statistics on energy inputs were used as a basis on which to estimate emissions.

Once the information has been collected, it must be transmitted in an appropriate format to the supervisory authorities. Monthly, quarterly or yearly reports will be required, according to circumstances. This information must then be entered into an accounting system recording the permits held by each agent and the transfers that have taken place. Advances in remote transmission and data processing now make all of these operations far easier to perform.

One final comment should be made with regard to systems for recording rights, emissions and transfers: it would be advisable, from an economic standpoint, to collect data relating not only to the physical quantities involved, but also to the price of transactions, even if the objectives of such data collection and the processing methods are different. This would confer an economically beneficial role on the data collection system, and not simply one of formal verification of compliance. The aim would be to compile a price index and other economic statistics about transactions. This solution echoes the fact that a market can only be efficient if agents are properly informed of equilibrium market prices. To safeguard the confidentiality of private transactions, information relating to the specific economic conditions under which individual transactions are made might not be made available to the public nor, more generally, to officials in the administration. Admittedly there may be some complications in that the price paid might in practice include various counterparts either in kind or of a specific nature and not simply a monetary payment. Problems such as these can be overcome. The alternative is allow economic data to be compiled by private brokers who take the initiative of regularly publishing price information based on the transactions for which they are the sole intermediaries. This issue merits further attention in that for existing schemes in the United States the recording system managed by the Federal EPA does not collect any data of an economic nature, letting that role to private initiatives.

Lastly, it should be noted that schemes in which permits are specified in relative values and those that make use of averaging both alter the way in which the monitoring system should be designed. To check whether performance complies with the rights issued, the compliance agencies must have access to detailed information regarding the economic activities of firms, such as sales figures for different models of product or the volume of inputs purchased during a given period, and not simply information on emission levels. Indeed, the determination of the permits held by agents depends upon the values taken by such indicators. This extension of the variables to be taken into account means that the inspection service must have access to the economic accounts of agents.

Compliance Checks and Incentives to Encourage Compliance with the Rules

Compliance with the emission or abstraction requirements of the permits held by agents can readily be checked provided that the information system is reliable. At regular intervals, at the end of each year for example, data on how agents have actually behaved are compared with the permit accounts maintained by the authorities and any failure to respect permit ceilings can readily be determined.

There are two factors that may need to be taken into account at this stage:

- *The availability of a grace period* in which to remedy the situation through purchases of permits, either from other agents willing to sell permits or from the supervisory agency itself should the latter have a reserve that it can use to sell permits at a set price (which under normal circumstance would be above the market rate) to agents who have failed to find partners for transfer transactions;
- *Initiation of sanction procedures.* As with any policy instrument, TPs can only function properly if it is credible and it can only be credible if agents who fail to comply with its rules are sanctioned sufficiently harshly to be discouraged from knowingly making use of this option.

There is a wide range of possible sanctions: forbidding future participation to transfers; automatic reduction in the quota allowance for the following period; payment of fines; obligation to fund compensatory activities aimed at enhancing the environment or the management of resources; temporary cessation of activities for a given period of time, equivalent to a temporary suspension of the licence to carry out the activity responsible for the emissions or abstractions; and lastly, legal proceedings and, in the event of a conviction, fines or prison sentences for those responsible. These sanctions may be imposed singly or as part of a raft of sanctions. The sanctions available under the Acid Rain Program in the United States include the payment of a dissuasive fine (over ten times the current market value of the permit) and the recovery of excesses on quotas for the following period. The situation is thereby restored in environmental terms while at the same time as the threat of a financial penalty serves as a disincentive.

What should be the strategy towards sanctions in this domain? Because in most cases the underlying rationale for permit transfer programmes is an economic one, sanctions too should primarily be of an economic rather than a penal nature; the former can be applied with far more flexibility and with greater ease than the latter which involve legal bodies with complex and often slow procedures and which, for this reason, should only be called upon in exceptional cases. Unlike the situation with traditional regulations, sanctions for non-compliance with the rules governing TP transactions should therefore be to commercial law rather than criminal law (Pearse, 1992). However, the application of sanctions must be credible and must therefore take place automatically without the need to instigate legal proceedings beforehand and without allowing for a discretionary implementation by an administrative authority.

If financial penalties are the mainstay of the system put in place to discourage possible misdemeanours, at what level should such penalties be placed? From an incentive viewpoint, a penalty has to be viewed as an instrument for discouraging evasion or negligence. The penalty is designed to ensure that the constraints expressed by permits are respected in their entirety. It is therefore necessary to reason in a way that takes account of both the probability that any misdemeanours will be detected and the size of the gain procured by not complying. If checks are made at highly infrequent intervals or it the offence cannot easily be detected, then a large fine must be imposed so that, despite the low chance of being caught, potential evaders prefer to comply with the rules. On the other hand, if infringements are readily apparent, then the penalty can be set at a lower level and yet nonetheless remain dissuasive.

At all events, it is advisable to use a system of proportional penalties that allow a distinction to be made between small and large overshoots on permits. Penalties must also be significantly higher than the profits which an agent might stand to gain from not complying with the rules of the system, although not so high as to bankrupt the agent. If the penalty were such that regardless of the overshoot or the infringement it would result in the agent ceasing his activities, the latter would find himself in a double or quits situation which, rather than encouraging him to comply with the regulations, might on the contrary prompt him to take a greater risk if he is not able to ensure a zero risk of non-compliance. The inspection authorities, too, might well be reluctant to impose sanctions if the consequences of such sanctions were to be so extreme.

Provisions to Promote Participation by Agents

Agents will only commit themselves to permit transfers if they have confidence in the rules put in place and are assured of not being penalised in the future for accepting to play the game and indirectly disclosing information about their technical capabilities of abating pollution or meeting abstraction limits. The trust of all agents, including the administration, in the rules and the stability of those rules are prerequisites for the satisfactory operation of the instrument. The same is true of the predictability of permit allowances for future periods. In programmes where allocations are periodically adjusted, it is essential that future allowances be determined on the basis of criteria that do not depend on abatement performance at previous stages of the programme. In the opposite case, abatement strategies will be perverted from the outset by speculations on the best means to maximise future allowances of TPs.

Agents must also have equal access to transfers, at modest transactions costs, without fear of being exposed to strategic manoeuvring on the market. To this end, it might be advisable for the permit transfer programme to be supervised by an independent administrative authority whose role would be to oversee the various aspects of its operation.

Depending upon the type of programme planned, it might be advisable to clearly set out the conditions under which agents would be allowed to participate voluntarily in programmes. The problem here is to be able to offer conditions that are attractive to new entrants but not penalising for current participants.

Two Examples of Transferable Permit Programmes

Having looked in turn at the various variables that enter into the design of a TP programme in order to illustrate the many options available to policy-makers, it might now be useful to examine a schematic illustration of the structure of the two programmes which are currently in operation in the United States and which have been referred to in passing in our discussion, namely the Federal Acid Rain Program for the transfer of SO_2 quotas and the RECLAIM Program in the Los Angeles area. Both of these programmes are aimed at tackling air pollution, but not the same type of air pollution in that the first programme addresses long-range acid pollution while the second is aimed at combating excessive levels of tropospheric ozone at the local and regional level around Los Angeles.

Table 3. **A Summary Comparison of the Acid Rain Programme and the RECLAIM Programme**

	Acid Rain Program	RECLAIM programme
1. Purpose and framework		
a. Policy goals	Long distance, diffuse acid deposition: 50% reduction in emissions (SO_2, NOx)	Local compliance with air quality standards: 70% reduction in ozone precursors
b. Political and economic context	Rather high reduction costs; uncertainty over benefits; conflicts over regional distribution	Very high reduction costs; large overshoots on standards; conflicts between economic growth and the environment
c. Overlapping regulations	Federal standards on ambient air quality and State limits on SO_2; public utility regulation	Federal standards on ambient air quality and State limits on PM10 and ozone
2. Field of operation		
a. Geographical scope	National	Local (L.A. district)
b. Pollutants targeted	SO_2, fairly uniform distribution	SOx and NOx, uneven distribution
c. Sources targeted	Large stationary sources	Stationary and partly mobile sources
d. Market structure		
Industries concerned	One only (power generation)	Several
Permit market	Competitive structure involving regulated utilities	Competitive structure with low concentration
3. Mode of operation		
a. Initial allocation	Grandfathering; numerous additional bonuses	Grandfathering; one type of bonus
b. Access for new entrants	Purchase of permits on the market; public reserve at high fixed price	Purchase of permits on the market; small reserve for firms with low emission levels but high job creation
c. Baseline	Average heat input over a historical period	Maximum emissions over a historical period
d. Transfer rules		
Temporal flexibility	No restrictions on banking; no borrowing	None
Spatial flexibility	No restriction	Two transfer zones
e. Monitoring and recording		
Emissions monitoring	Continuous and mandatory, using sensors at each source	Continuous using sensors at each source, mandatory for two thirds of sources
Emissions reporting	Quarterly	Daily, monthly or quarterly
Public information on emissions	Yearly	Yearly
Reporting of transfers	Mandatory solely when permits are used by purchaser	Mandatory solely when permits are used by purchaser
Administration of emission inventories and permit accounts	Via a public agency	Via a public agency
f. Enforcement		
Reconciliation of emissions and permits	Yearly, with a grace period of 30 days	Yearly, with a grace period of two months
Financial penalties	$2000 a tonne, applied automatically	Up to $500 per infringement, not automatic
Deduction from the budget for the following period	Yes, 1 for 1	Yes, 1 for 1
g. Market initialisation		
Auctions	Mandatory yearly auction of 2.8% of annual basic allowances, open to all	Private and voluntary auctions at regular intervals, open to all
h. Scope for voluntary participation	Yes	Yes
4. Policy process		
a. Public participation in the design	Very active; wide-ranging and close consultations with the various parties; debates in Congress	Very active; in-depth discussions organised by the agency responsible for air quality (SCAQMD)
b. Administrative requirement	100 officials	From 30 to 100 officials
c. Timetable	Introduced in two mandatory stages	Immediate mandatory application
5. Legislative status	Provisions set out in a federal law (CAAA 1990), including the initial allocation of allowances; allowances are administrative authorisations, not property rights	Local programme endorsed by the State of California and the Federal Agency for Environmental Protection; allowances are administrative authorisations, not property rights

This table is based on that established by Schwarze and Zapfel (2000), to which a number of adjustments and additions have been made.

Notes

1. Dales (1968*b*) himself pointed out that emission allowance markets were not true markets because the supply of permits or quotas, set by the authorities, did not respond to price signals; demand alone adjusted, meaning that the instrument was simply a special administrative instrument.
2. This was the case with the Davis Plan introduced in 1968 to reduce salmon fishing capacity in British Columbia. The plan ultimately failed to meet its objectives in that capacities nonetheless increased. In accordance with proposals which the author had put forward shortly before (Pearse, 1980), the 1982 Pearse report recommended the introduction of transferable catch quotas.
3. Under the RECLAIM programme in the district of Los Angeles, the opposite situation arose in that part of the permits allocated were "usable but non-transferable". The reason for this was that firms received an allocation of TPs which in some cases included additional non-transferable quotas designed to take account of the peculiarities of their situation with regard to the historical reference chosen for the basic allocation (Harrison, 1999).
4. The value to the bidder of goods with private value depends solely on the private information he has on his own particular circumstances. This corresponds to cases in which goods are destined for use solely by their owner. For goods with common value, all bidders assign to them the same value in that these goods may subsequently be resold and there is a market in which they can be sold. In the event that there is a liquid secondary market, TPs will fall into the second category.
5. Over periods in excess of five years, for instance, economic agents may anticipate changes in the legislature, with power coming to lie with groups more attentive to their interests.
6. As in the case of New York State, which feared damage to some of the nature reserves it manages and appealed against the EPA programme of tradable SO_2 permits to the Court of Appeal in Washington. The appeal was not upheld.

Chapter 3

Implementation Issues and Constraints

TPs are not the only economic instrument that can be used to implement environmental policy, nor are they the sole policy instruments available. This family of instruments must therefore compete with others whenever a new policy is required or when existing policies need to be amended. In recent years in particular, the business sector and government authorities have given long and careful consideration to instruments such as negotiated voluntary agreements, environmental quality labels or certification of the environmental management of industrial sites (Dente, 1995; OECD, 1999*b*).

It is therefore necessary to identify the main issues informing the choices that must be made by policy-makers and the administration. Environmental issues are not the only issues that must be taken into account, even if they provide the initial justification for the actions undertaken. The willingness of decision-makers to opt for TPs rather than another instrument will depend upon the way in which TPs can accommodate these issues in addressing given types of environmental problem and objective. The issues in question are the competitiveness of firms, the degree to which the new instrument is compatible with the institutional framework and instruments already in place, and the distributive aspects and social acceptability of TPs.

Issues Relating to Competitiveness and Market Power

The Environment and Competitiveness

One of the principal findings of the economic analysis of environmental issues is that in order to ensure that competition leads to collective economic efficiency, each economic agent must be made to take account of all the costs (commitment of private and collective resources) that ensue from his decisions. In particular, it is only when the external costs to the environment have been properly internalised by agents through appropriate mechanisms that competition can pave the way for economic efficiency. When the external costs generated are not the same across economic agents, it is justifiable from an economic standpoint for public intervention to impose different charges to them through application of the polluter-pays-principle (OECD, 1975). Such a policy cannot be said to be a source of distortion of competition since it is the very initial situation in which agents disregard their external environmental costs that is economically distorted. Admittedly, it may modify the prevailing conditions of competition between firms and in doing so adversely affect the immediate competitiveness of the firms generating the highest external costs. This holds true both for competition between firms operating in the same branch and for the balance between different branches or sectors of activity. Obviously transitional costs of adjustment will have to be taken into account when a new policy is introduced.

Partial and asymmetrical application of the principle of internalising external costs between competing firms would obviously lead to a distortion of competition which would be damaging to firms that take proper account of their external costs and, because of this, would make it harder to meet environmental objectives. It is for this reason that adoption of the principle of internalising external costs by the international community has a key role to play in establishing normal conditions for international competition. This does not mean to say, however, that the same environmental requirements and standards should apply in all countries. Where external costs incurred are local by nature, it is the preferences of the local population which should serve as the ultimate reference for trade-offs and these preferences may differ from one country to another. This is not the case for global phenomena such as climate change in that the impact that greenhouse gas emissions have on climate is unrelated to the location where such emissions originate.

Competitiveness has become a central issue both in the general public debate and in the debate over environmental policy, and yet retrospective analyses of the possible linkages between competitiveness and the severity of environmental policy have so far failed to demonstrate the existence of a statistically significant link (Adams, 1998; Johnstone, 1999) even though links have been shown to exist in certain individual cases. This does not mean to say that such a link may not arise in the future with regard to problems of far greater economic impact such as global warming. So how do matters stand with TPs?

It is with TP schemes that the risk of problems arising with regard to competitiveness, distortion of competition and the arbitrary relocation of activities is likely to be the smallest. This results from the way TPs change the opportunities to which agents have access and their decision problems. For example, if two countries adopt regulatory regimes of differing stringency, they effectively impose different costs on their respective firms. This may modify the respective competitiveness of those firms. If international trade in TPs can emerge on the same regulatory background, the advantages gained by firms benefiting from the most favourable regime will be comparatively lower in that, through transfers, their potential for abating pollution at lower cost will allow firms in the other country to avoid the high costs that a rigid system would impose on them.

Even if there is no international trade in permits, TPs can have a favourable impact on economic competitiveness, compared with regulatory approaches, by combining three modes of action: (1) reduction of short and medium-term costs within the area in which permits are allowed to circulate; (2) stimulation of technical innovation in the longer term, leading to increased productivity; (3) reduction of macroeconomic distortions arising from taxation in cases where permits are sold to economic agents and the resultant tax revenue is used to reduce those taxes which distort the economy the most. It may be noted that these three modes of action are not exclusive to TPs since they can also be achieved through an approach based on incentive taxes.

In order to gain greater insight into the final impact of TPs on competitiveness, it would now be worth taking a closer look at the variables through which this instrument can work.

Key Variables with Regard to Competitiveness

A distinction may be drawn between the short-term impact of TPs on market equilibrium and competitiveness, when plant and technology are deemed to be already acquired, and the long-term impact when technical innovation and capital mobility are taken into account. These two types of impact will be generated through different mechanisms.

Economic Impact of the Possibility of Trading Emission Permits

The first way in which TPs can influence market conditions is through the very mechanism of trading. In the following discussion, sketched in a partial equilibrium framework, it is assumed that the instrument will initially apply to all competitors. The second part of the discussion will consider competition between firms whose facilities are located in areas subject to different environmental regimes.

Formation of a Price on the Permit Market which Reflects the Intensity of the Rationing Constraint But Not its Mode of Introduction

In a partial equilibrium and under certain conditions (i.e. no income effect changing demand functions) the choice of an initial rule of allocation of rights on some good will not affect the economic equilibrium of the market (prices and quantities supplied and demanded) of that good, provided that the good in question can be sold. This outcome was demonstrated in the pioneering work of Coase (1960). It applies to TPs as well, as long as they are transferable. The main conditions required for such an outcome are that property and usage rights be clearly defined, that transaction costs be low enough to be negligible and that a competitive market for TPs produce a benchmark price valid for all agents. So, what factors determine the market equilibrium of TPs? From the viewpoint of agents, the basic outline of the situation is as follows: in order to reduce their emissions to a level that matches the number of permits allocated to them, agents can opt for various solutions whose costs will vary accordingly; trading will therefore be initiated in order to exploit differences in cost from one agent to another and as a result of such trading a benchmark price will eventually emerge. For agents buying permits, this price places a ceiling on the unit cost of the pollution reduction effort that they will undertake. In standard flexible conditions the marginal cost of abatement accepted by these agents will be of equal value with price of TPs on the market. For those selling permits, this price also defines the benchmark for setting the maximum cost at which it would be reasonable for them to reduce emissions and thereby generate a surplus of permits that they could then sell. This equilibrium price of TPs, of equal value with marginal abatement cost of all competitors, is therefore only determined by the marginal cost functions for abatement of pollution or pressure on resources and the overall environmental constraint imposed by the authorities, which expresses itself as a rationing constraint on agents.

If they are rational, it is the market price for permits that all agents, regardless of their initial allocation of permits and the rule for initial allocation, will take into account when taking decisions as technical managers of installations and operators on the permit market, either as potential buyers or as potential sellers. This means that under competitive conditions the market price for permits is impervious to the rules for initial allocation (amount of individual endowments, free or charged allocation) once the overall constraint (a cap or the aggregate of individual regulatory authorisations) is fixed, unless there were to be significant impacts on the general equilibrium of the economy. Such impacts might arise in theory were the allocation of permits, through firms' profits and the remuneration of shareholders and perhaps employees too, to lead to wide-scale redistribution of income within the firm, which in practice would seem to be no more than a text-book hypothesis with regard to most, if not all, TP systems considered in this study.

It would therefore be illusory to believe that the equilibrium price on the permit market, and thus the economic cost of the environmental constraint, could be reduced by distributing permits free of charge. The outcome of free distribution of permits might be to compensate some agents by limiting the financial impact of that constraint on their profits, while in contrast other agents would have to support both an increase in the price of the products they purchase, as a result of the introduction of the environmental constraint, and the perpetuation of existing economic distortions of a fiscal nature which would penalise them both as workers and as consumers.

A Downstream Product Market that is Impervious to the Initial Rule for Permit Allocation

Even if a firm has received a permit free of charge, the use of that permit has a cost that for the holder is equal to the profit he could make by selling it on the market. TPs are new valuable assets and will be considered as such by agents making use of them, whatever way of access is decided on. So in a competitive environment all firms subject to a TP regime would integrate the same marginal cost for a permit into their production costs, either as a direct cost if they have to buy it or as an opportunity cost if the permit has been granted for free by the authorities (see Box 13). The value accounted for decision-making being the same regardless of the rule for initial allocation, there is no reason why the respective market shares in product markets, which reflect the respective production cost functions of agents, would be affected in the short run. The same is true of the various economic agents operating in downstream markets (consumer industries, end consumers) who are wholly indifferent to the choice of an initial allocation rule for agents upstream, apart from the fact that if permits were to be distributed

Box 13. **Impacts of Free Versus Charged Allocation of TPs on Products Costs**

Assuming an initial allocation of TPs made free of charge to firm *i* for an amount G_i on an historical basis, not related to future behaviour of the firm, it is possible to contrast two viewpoints on cost impacts and pricing of products. The direct financial (I) approach only considers direct financial flows; a free allocation G_i save a financial expenditure of the same amount; the greater G_i is, the lower is the financial impact of production costs. The economic way of thinking (II) considers G_i as an initial asset that can be used or sold on the market. Using it has an opportunity cost in proportion to the market value of TPs. At the margin, the cost of using a permit is determined by the market price of this permit, not the amount of G_i.

With (I), the cost function can be written as: $F_i(q_i,b_i,G_i) = C_i(q_i) + A_i(b_iE_{i0}) + Q_i(p[(1 - b_i)E_{i0} - G_i])$

with : $C_i(q_i)$ the production cost, excluding environmental components, as a function of product output q_i

$A_i(b_iE_{i0})$ the abatement cost as a function of the initial level of emissions E_{i0} and the abatement rate or level of effort b_i, with $\sum_i(1 - b_i)E_{io} \leq \sum_i G_i$

$Q_i\ (p[(1 - b)E_{i0} - G_i])$ the expenditure to buy additional permits at price p to cover emissions not covered by G_i.

This financial cost function (I) depends on G_i. The conclusion seems to be clear-cut: the allocation rule influences the production cost of firm *i* and its immediate competitiveness on the product market. This is not the economic view, because this direct financial approach is forgetting to take account of the loss of income resulting from the use of TPs by firm i to cover its own emissions. So, for a profit-seeking firm, the cost function (II) can be written as:

$F'_i(q,b,G_i) = C_i(q_i) + A_i(b_iE_{i0}) + Q'_i(p[(1 - b_i)E_{i0} - G_i] + pG_i)$, which comes to:

$F'_i(q,b,G_i) = C_i(q) + A_i(bE_{i0}) + Q'_i(p(1 - b)E_{i0})$,

(II) is definitely non dependent on G_i. Each unit of TPs has a value and using it implies a cost for the firm which is to be reflected in the price offered on the market by all firms concerned. A free allocation comes to a gift of assets, but as is shown by property rights on land, this does not mean that using it is without cost for the owner, insofar there is a market value for it (Koutstaal, 1997). In this view, auctioning TPs will not affect costing procedures and the market equilibrium on a competitive product market.

through an auctioning procedure those agents could benefit from reductions in taxes or charges introduced in order to maintain budget neutrality.

Sensitivity of Economic Equilibria to Transaction Costs and Asymmetries in Environmental Protection Regimes

Respective market shares and the new equilibrium prices in product markets may be affected by transaction costs if the latter are significant (Stavins, 1995) and also by the asymmetries that geographical or size limitations to the application of TPs might introduce into competition between firms.

If there are transaction costs, then potentially attractive transactions will not be completed. As a result, the cost of strategies towards compliance with the emissions covered by permit allocations will remain uneven, at the margin, from one firm to another. The rules for the initial allocation of permits will therefore have an impact both on the final distribution of abatement efforts and on the marginal costs taken into account in agents' decisions. It is therefore when the public authorities introduce administrative measures (preliminary authorisations, various restrictions in time and space) which have the effect of raising transaction costs and preventing the equalisation of marginal costs, even if the such measures are well-intentioned (which does not necessarily mean that they are well-founded), that such measures will adversely affect the economic efficiency of TPs and then the competitiveness of firms, that will have to bear higher costs than it possible for them to obtain with a more fluent organisation.

Furthermore, the production prices of producers located outside the territorial perimeter of the TP programme, who would therefore not be integrated as participants into the TP system, would continue to reflect solely their internal production costs and not the external environmental costs addressed by this programme. This situation would lead to the emergence of a production price differential that would be to the disadvantage of those firms participating in the TP system, regardless of the rule for initial allocation applicable within that perimeter. Both the short-term competitiveness and the respective market shares of those firms would therefore be affected. But this impact is the result of the environmental programme, not the one of TPs, which would lessen as much as possible this impact.

If the production price of firms that do not participate imposes itself, through competition, as the market price within the TP area, then it is the cash-flow of participating firms that will decline and, subsequently, the remuneration of the factors of production (capital, labour) concerned. Depending upon the quantitative scale of the phenomenon, this situation may lead to losses of market share or even to closures of facilities. Even in such cases, the outcome is due to a process of adjustment relating to a new economic situation generated, not by TPs, but by the asymmetrical introduction of the environmental constraint itself[1]; once the adjustment has been made, the situation may stabilise, other resources of competitiveness (innovation) may be mobilised in order to establish a more favourable equilibrium or, if the magnitude of phenomena is really significant, macroeconomic adjustments (modification of exchange rate parities) may emerge and mitigate the impact.

These findings come as no surprise. If some competitors are able to avoid environmental costs, their competitive position in relation to other firms will be improved in terms of costs, even if this effect may be attenuated by other non-cost components of competitiveness such as brand image[2]. Distributing permits free of charge would not be a solution to this type of loss of competitiveness, even if it could attenuate the financial impact on the accounts of the firms concerned. In contrast, they would not benefit from any reduction in taxes or charges that the initial sale of permits could afford.

Impacts that Depend upon the Competitive Structure of the Product Market

In order to gain a better insight into the possible impact of TPs on competitiveness, it is necessary to take account of the competitive structure of the activity in question, and introduce the following distinctions:

- competitive environments in which all firms are forced to consider prices as given (price-taker firms), compared with conditions of imperfect competition in which prices are strategic variables in the control of at least a number of firms (price-maker firms);
- symmetrical contexts in which all firms are subject to the same programme and the same environmental constraint, compared with asymmetrical contexts in which solely firms located within a certain geographical area must and can participate in a TP programme.

For individual firms, the economic impact would also depend on the margin each firm would have to pass on cost increases, induced by the environmental constraint, to product prices or the prices of certain factors of production or certain forms of intermediate consumption. This would depend upon the degree of imperfect competition and the price-elasticities of supply and demand for the products in question. If supply is inelastic but demand elastic, a monopoly would preserve its market position by maintaining the previous price and by absorbing the cost increase through lower profits. If demand is inelastic, it would be able to pass on cost increases through retail prices.

The upstream/downstream relationship in the transmission of the price effect associated with TPs will play a central role in the distribution of rents in that firms which can transmit the price effect to their suppliers and customers will be able to maintain, or even increase, their profits, while those exposed to competition from firms that are not subject to the environmental policy or to a flexible demand, will have to agree to lower their profits in order to maintain market share or accept a reduction in those market shares. Analysis of these upstream/downstream relations is important in order to decide at which point in the productive chain the environmental constraint must be introduced in cases of general pollution arising from the consumption of certain widely utilised goods, for example CO_2 emissions resulting from the consumption of fossil fuels. If the aim is to spread a price effect across the economy, it would be advisable to introduce the constraint at the point where the price effect can actually be transmitted.

At the international level, the ultimate economic impact of domestic TP programmes will primarily depend upon the degree of fragmentation or integration of the markets for industrial products and, notably, the density of international trade and the influence of transport costs[3].

Impact of the Rule for Initial Allocation on Investment and Innovation in a Competitive Environment

The importance of the initial allocation variable, as demonstrated in the previous section, warrants a more detailed examination of how it may impacts profits, investments and innovation.

The initial allocation (permits issued free of charge or sold to users) directly determines an income effect (transfer of revenue between agents, in this particular case between the State and firms, and indirectly between firms) which may be quite substantial. The difference between allocating permits free of charge and selling them may be as great as that between a regulatory instrument and an incentive tax. This income effect only has a direct impact on the profitability of the existing productive systems of firms, but as discussed in the previous section, in the short term has no significant impact on the market shares for their products. However, there may be indirect and longer-term impacts on economic equilibria and competitiveness.

Taking a free allocation as a benchmark for making comparisons, auctioning or selling TPs another way will reduce current profits of firms. That reduction could primarily have three types of impact:

- T*he closure of certain facilities* in cases where, solely by virtue of the rule for initial allocation, it proved to be more advantageous to firms to close certain facilities rather than to continue to produce. Even if such an extreme decision were to be taken, it would only concern the most polluting and least efficient facilities, which generally tend to be the oldest ones. The initial investment in such facilities should therefore, as a general rule, already be almost fully amortised. In practice, therefore, firms would only have to bear the variable costs. In view of this, it is highly implausible that a large-scale closure of facilities could be attributable to the decision to charge for the initial permit allocation. In most cases, such facilities would have been closed anyway.

- A *relative fall in the share value of firms which have to buy their permits* compared to that of those to whom permits would be allocated free of charge or who do not need permits, since the stock market value is considered to reflect the capitalisation of the profits expected from exploitation of the productive capital during the active life of the firm; accordingly, the income of assets of the shareholders concerned would decline compared with those of the shareholders in firms benefiting from a free allowance or not concerned by the programme.

- A *relative reduction in the self-financing capacity of firms* and, in consequence, a change in their access to borrowing or to the capital market. To finance the same projects, firms obliged to purchase all their permits would have to borrow more and pay more interests than they would have had to had they received them free of charge; in addition to higher financial charges, they would then also incur a higher risk premium due to a change in the structure of balance sheet liabilities. This lowering of the self-financing capacity should in particular have a knock-on effect on investment in R&D, one of the variables that affects future competitiveness.

The impact on investment capacity depends to a large extent on the degree of imperfection in the financial market, since it is the imperfections in this market that lend a specific weight to the financing constraint. The greater the imperfections, leading for example to *de facto* credit rationing, the greater the account taken in risk in the financial analysis of the firm's balance sheet (gearing ratio) and the more the self-financing capacity of firms becomes a strategic resource for the funding of profitable investment projects, then the better the position of firms capable of generating high cash-flows from existing activities. Thus the factors influencing long-term competitiveness (development of new capacities, modernisation of existing capacities, redeployment into other areas of activity and support for R&D programmes) will all the more strongly be affected by self-financing capacities the greater the degree of imperfection.

In contrast, if capital can readily be raised on the financial market and if investors are capable of focusing more on the potential profitability of future projects than on the performance of existing activities, then the adverse impact of a permit auctioning system on profits would be of no consequence for future competitiveness.

To complete this picture, account must lastly be taken of the provisions set out in the rules for permit access applicable to new installations. Should new entrants and new installations enjoy the same conditions for access to permits as existing installations or would they be subject to specific conditions? There are several issues involved here.

- If the access to permits granted to existing and new facilities is asymmetrical, with the former receiving a free allocation and the latter having to buy permits, the benefit of the scarcity rent assigned to existing installations through the free distribution of permits does not extend to new investment, which should therefore not be biased since the cost of the environmental constraint to be supported is the same whoever invests. This is the critical point: conditions for new investment should be the same for all firms and all similar programmes in various regions. The fact that existing firms have a higher self-financing capacity, because they receive permits free of charge, than would have been the case had auctioning been introduced would not in itself constitute a sufficient reason to encourage them to invest in projects for which there is no economic justification. If the capital market is fluid, and if technology can readily be transferred, then the same future investment will nonetheless be made by one firm or another regardless of the profitability and past financial capacities of the various firms concerned.

- The distribution of additional remuneration to shareholders in firms whose existing installations would benefit from a free allocation of permits undoubtedly has distributive effects. But does it have an impact on the competitiveness of the firms present in the market? While the propensity of shareholders to make profitable investments by taking calculated risks is also shared between the shareholders of different competing companies, there is no reason to believe that allowing some of them to make additional profits would help to improve competitiveness of some firms rather than others. Here again, the main factor that will determine investment in plant is projected future profitability.

- Long-term competitiveness undoubtedly depends upon the innovative process that allows factor productivity to be enhanced and that integrates different constraints and objectives of a general nature such as protection of the environment. If it is accepted that an innovation is the outcome of not only the availability of financing capacity but also the economic attractiveness of that innovation and the interest that firms have in exploiting it, then the auctioning procedure would seem to be superior to the free allocation of permits. Because the free allocation of permits may be viewed, in part, as the attribution of a scarcity rent to certain agents, those receiving such a rent have no interest in undertaking actions that might ultimately reduce it. This would be the case of innovations whose diffusion would lower the market value of permits. Solely appropriable innovations such as private goods, whose diffusion could be restricted, would be attractive to those receiving a rent, which would therefore be a limiting factor. In contrast, innovation would be a far more attractive general option for firms if the latter had to acquire all or a significant proportion of their emission permits in order to be able to continue operating their installations.

It would appear from this analysis that the impact of initial allocation methods on the economic equilibrium and competitiveness of firms should be far less than is sometimes claimed. The scale of the impact will in fact depend upon the conditions of competition in the permit market and in the market for the products of firms participating in the TP programme, and even more so on the degree of imperfection in the capital market (stock market information on the outlook for investments) and the financial market (access to borrowing). If the conditions of competition in the different types of market are satisfactory, the income-effects of the choice of a rule for initial allocation should have a negligible impact on short and medium-term market equilibria, and also on the choice of investment that will determine future competitiveness. This outcome will only be achieved, however, if investors are all subject to the same rule of access to permits for new investments.

The greatest impacts on competitiveness may be expected from asymmetries in environmental protection regimes between different regions or countries. Indeed it is not so much the inequalities in environmental protection levels that is of importance as the fact that these regimes cannot be integrated into a common operating system. If firms located in areas where environmental protection measures are less stringent could enter the permit market in areas where such protection is higher, the competitive biases would in large part be eliminated because all firms would base their decisions on the same given benchmark: the market price of permits.

The Influence of Imperfect Competition

Under conditions of imperfect competition, when producers or consumers are able to exert an influence on market prices, the rules for initial permit allocation may prompt firms to modify their strategy.

This may occur if there is monopolistic competition in the permit market. If a monopoly on the permit market receives an allowance that is greater than it ultimately needs once its strategy of use of permits has been adjusted in view of their market value, it would find itself in a selling position. It would therefore be in its interest to adopt an emissions policy that is non-optimal for the community, i.e. excessive emissions, in order to restrict the supply of permits and thereby force prices up. In contrast, if the allowance fails to meet all its needs, it would be in its interests to make larger reductions in emission rates than the standard optimum in order to restrict its demand and thereby force permit prices down (Hahn, 1984). The authorities called upon to regulate the activity of potential monopolies in such a permit market might therefore see the initial allocation rule as an opportunity to create an incentive for firms to voluntarily reduce emissions below the static optimum, inasmuch this would prepare the way for achieving a dynamic optimum on a trajectory marked by steady increases in the

Box 14. **A Case where it may be Economically Advantageous to Choose Non-Transferable Quotas**

A comparison is made here of an approach based on absolute, non-transferable quotas and one based on transferable quotas in the case where the structure of the product market is a Cournot duopoly[4]. With non-transferable emission quotas defined in absolute terms, if product technology is uniform, the most efficient agent in terms of emissions reduction is encouraged to achieve a higher rate of unit clean-up, since the clean-up costs are lower. This allows the agent to increase production and gain market share from his competitor in the product market, who must bear a higher average cost of abatement. This approach based on absolute and non-transferable quotas therefore creates a new balance in market share in favour of the agent with the lowest clean-up costs. However, because of the discrepancies between quota allocations, the marginal costs of emissions reduction are not evened out between the two competitors, which constitutes an economic loss.

Authorising quota trading in this context has two outcomes: on the one hand, the improved efficiency of the sub-problem of optimising the clean-up effort; but on the other hand an opposing trend whereby the least efficient agent in terms of clean-up regains market share in the product market at the expense of the competitor who is more efficient in terms of clean-up, since the latter finds it more advantageous to transfer a portion of his quota to the former. By means of this acquisition, the least efficient firm lowers its average abatement cost and can act more aggressively on the product market than would be the case if quotas were not transferable.

In other words, the freedom to trade quotas attenuates the impact of the initial difference in efficiency from the standpoint of clean-up between the two competitors and allows the least efficient firm to better defend its position in the product market. If this outcome is extrapolated, it would mean that TPs would be likely to have a lesser impact on the conditions of competition prevailing in product markets prior to the introduction of the environmental constraint than approaches based on non-transferable quotas.

stringency of the environmental constraint. All that would be needed to do would be to allocate to firms in a monopoly position a number of permits that falls significantly short of their requirements; obviously such an approach would only be valid in the case of free administrative allocation of permits. As clever as this approach would be, it could meet significant difficulties during the policy process because monopolies generally have political resources to be preferentially heard by the public authorities.

In several papers (1994, 1997*a*, 1997*b*) Sartzetakis has examined the interactions between permit and product markets. In one case he shows that under certain imperfect product market conditions it would be wise in economic terms to voluntarily restrict trading in emissions permits, even if permits are traded on a competitive basis (Sartzetakis, 1997*b*) (see Box 14).

It is by no means easy to take imperfect competition accurately into account, however, in that the outcomes that need to be integrated depend upon a variety of factors. In practical terms, this might argue in favour of organising regulatory systems by branch in order to reflect the structure of product markets. In addition to the level of information which regulators would need to have at their disposal in order to be to able to intervene in an informed manner in each branch, this type of compartmentalisation of TP trading would lead to significant losses of efficiency and would preclude the emergence of a large competitive TP market that could be expected if trading were allowed across branches and sectors. It might therefore be wiser to preserve the competitive nature of the TP market than attempt to fine tune the product market.

Impact of Prospects for Fiscal Redeployment

The above considerations must not divert attention from the fact that the income effect of the choice of rule for initial allocation will necessarily vary according to the fiscal strategy for using additional resources generated by auctioning. This includes the prospect for a general redeployment of taxation.

If the scope for fiscal redeployment is taken into account, two alternatives emerge (Johnstone, 1999*b*; Cramton and Kerr, 1998):

- *The initial allocation is free*. The scarcity rents arising from the introduction of the environmental constraint, related to marginal cost of compliance with the constraint, are assigned to firms, and not to consumers or tax-payers who nonetheless benefit from the improvement to the environment. In this respect, the procedure tends to increase the financial capacity of firms; on the other hand, the instrument does not make it possible to improve taxation and reduce the existing fiscal distortions affecting all agents. According to the firm, one effect will outweigh the other; however, the outcome for certain groups of firms (firms that are major energy consumers, heavy industry, fossil-fired power plants, labour-intensive firms) and society as a whole (variations in welfare surplus of employees, shareholders, consumers and the State as representative of third parties) is unlikely to be the same;
- A *charge is levied for the initial allocation, preferably through an auction procedure*. Scarcity rents are recovered by the public authorities which have various means at their disposal either for redistributing rents between different categories of the population, or for reducing the community charges and taxes that are mostly responsible for economic distortions; the gains in competitiveness in different sectors of the economy may be greater than the loss of competitiveness of those sectors emitting the highest intensity of pollutants; this is the so-called double-dividend theory.

Admittedly there is also a third option which is to use an auctioning procedure to overcome the arbitrary nature of an initial allocation based on administrative or political criteria and to encourage the emergence of a benchmark price and thereby return the financial income from such a sale on a neutral basis in terms of pollutant emissions (for instance turnover or value added) to the participating firms.

In all cases, two major conclusions may be drawn:

- Whatever the option chosen, it is the combined result of the rule of initial allocation and fiscal restitution or redeployment which must be assessed in order to determine the net distributive impact and possible consequences for the competitiveness of firms, with results that will vary according to the type of firm and sector, e.g. whether or not they are major emitters of pollutants;

- The difference in the financial impact on firms between free distribution of permits and sale by auction depends upon how ambitious the environmental or resource programme's objectives are, that is to say in practical terms the rate of reduction of emissions or intake imposed on firms. If the rate required is relatively low, the weight of expenditure on abatement remains modest, the greatest financial burden lies in expenditure on permits in the event of a sale by auction. In contrast, the financial issues at stake with auctioned permits become less important the larger the reductions to be applied and the greater the differences in cost functions between economic agents, in which case expenditure on abatement will outweigh any expenditure on initial purchases of permits, whereas the flexibility afforded by the possibility of trading permits offers major savings in abatement costs (Johnstone, 1999*b*).

Issues Relating to Compatibility with Institutional Framework for Public Policies and with Existing Instruments

Three Problems of Compatibility

A new policy does not simply appear out of thin air. Even if it is designed to deal with a new problem for which there is still no public action, there nonetheless exist constitutional principles and a general legislative and administrative basis on which it will have to be founded. When the aim is to improve an existing policy, the constraint may be all the stronger in that while changes may undoubtedly need to be made, the latter must nonetheless be precisely matched to the components of the pre-existing system that are to be retained. Lastly, it is possible that public policy may attempt to find a durable mix of different instruments in order to exploit some of their complementarities. In view of this, a distinction needs to be drawn beforehand between three different issues of compatibility, namely:

- *The compatibility of* TPs *with the general requirements of public law*, the organisation of institutions and the division of areas of responsibility between the latter; this will be referred to as the problem of "institutional compatibility", a term that should clearly be understood in the broad sense;
- *The compatibility of* TPs *with the various components of the regulatory regimes in place*; this analysis must be able to determine the scale of the changes to be made to the organisation in place in order to be able to operate the new instrument and mutually adjust the elements from different sources that must now be integrated into the same system; the terms in which this problem of compatibility are couched will vary according to whether the environmental problem to be resolved has already been addressed by a policy that made use of certain instruments (regulations or taxes) or whether it is a new problem that allows greater leeway for designing a new regulatory system according to the objectives pursued; this problem will be known as that of "transitional compatibility";
- *The compatibility of* TPs *with other instruments such as taxes and duties or negotiated voluntary agreements, within permanent combinations* and no longer transitional compromises; this problem will be referred to as that of "combinatory compatibility".

The Challenges of Institutional Compatibility

This problem of compatibility is fundamental and concerns the very possibility of adding TPs to the policy instruments used in a given country. The question is quite simply whether the TP systems envisaged can overcome the legal hurdle or whether the legal system of a country and the principles and concepts on which the various systems of TPs are based are fundamentally incompatible. Thus, the principles of the equality of citizens in the eyes of tax law, non-transferability or sale of administrative permits, the non-appropriation of *res communis* or the individual's right to a healthy environment might be major, if not insuperable, obstacles which might lead to the rejection of TPs at an early stage in the policy-making process, or at least make it impossible to use certain procedures that would nonetheless be of economic interest. There are several examples of such incompatibility:

- The auctioning of permits would run counter to a principle that administrative permits cannot be sold in countries where that principle applies;
- The principle of the equality of citizens in terms of tax might preclude the partial use of the auctioning procedure for some agents or sectors only, whereas others would benefit directly or indirectly from a free allocation of permits;
- In countries that have adopted the principle of non-compensation for public service requirements and restrictions on property rights, the legal certainty of allocated permits might be adversely affected in that the public authorities could easily introduce different restrictions on the use of such permits at a later date while disregarding the economic losses that such action would entail for the agents entitled to permits.

However, in most cases in which incompatibility with basic principles has been identified in the first analysis, it would seem that it is possible to find means of safeguarding not only these principles but also the future prospects for TPs, provided that there is a political will to achieve such a result[5]. Thus in the United States, the fact that several legislative texts have clearly specified that emission permits were not property rights has not prevented different TP systems from being developed. However, the compromises that may have to be made in order to achieve such a result may significantly restrict the deployment of the instrument and may prevent it from realising its full potential.

The Challenges of Transitional Compatibility

The main challenge with regard to "transitional compatibility" is firstly a political and economic one. How can the costs of adaptation be minimised, that is to say how can legislative amendments, administrative changes, organisational reform and the creation of new agencies, notably monitoring and information systems, be limited without diminishing the properties of TPs that make them attractive and justify their introduction? These two objectives are usually diametrically opposed.

Attempting to graft TPs onto a system that is still governed by a multitude of regulatory requirements and limit-values (concerning the quality of the environment, emissions, production processes) on the basis of concepts such as the "best available technology", in accordance with lists drawn up by the administration of the technical processes to be employed, all of which being subject to a prior authorisation procedure for each transfer, might therefore be feasible on paper but in reality would offer virtually no flexibility to decentralised economic agents nor any significant economic gain. Experiences in a number of countries, such as the United States and Switzerland, have shown that over a period of several years the formal authorisation of permit trading within local areas sometimes has not resulted in any such transaction taking place (Smith, 1999; Jeanrenaud, 1999).

Note should be taken of the following limiting factors in particular.

Existing Regulations Focused on Process Standardisation

A major obstacle to the introduction of TPs arises when regulations are organised through administrative orders regarding technology to be used and not on standards relating to the emission or the release of pollutants to the environment. A permit trading system is only feasible if the good to be traded can be quantified. It is therefore necessary to begin by drawing up quantified unit-values before it is possible to consider incorporating TPs into the existing system, that is to say a shift away from process standards towards emissions or performance standards.

The most practical way of proceeding in terms of the rationale for operation of a TP system is to draw up regulatory requirements in terms of absolute quantities, that is to say quotas that are valid for a given period of time, since quotas can be traded directly. This does not prevent quotas being allocated by applying a formula based on a unit emissions rate multiplied by a level of activity observed over a historical period in the past.

However, the experience with the introduction of lead-free petrol in the United States (Nussbaum, 1992), in particular, clearly shows that it is not necessary for the initial requirements to be set out in absolute terms. Setting targets in unit rates is perfectly acceptable provided that the activity variable can be more or less predicted *ex ante* and accurately determined *ex post*, for example at the end of each period. However, in such an approach, trading as such is only about absolute quantities. This can create uncertainty in the minds of potential traders: the vendor, because he does not know in advance exactly what he can sell, since that will depend upon the trend in his activity over the entire period; and the buyer because he does not know precisely *ex ante* what his needs will be, which will only become apparent at the end of the period when he will know exactly what his level of activity has been. This problem is all the more pressing in that the activity in question is volatile and dependent upon an unstable economic climate.

Maintaining Constraints on the Technological Processes Used

The purpose of TPs is to allow decentralised agents to enjoy some flexibility in the choice of the best strategies towards achieving a given environmental performance. Such flexibility is a necessary condition for these agents to be able to minimise the cost of achieving a given environmental objective for society. In line with their earlier practices, however, administrations have attempted to maintain specific requirements regarding the technologies to be used, undoubtedly because they saw this as a reassuring guarantee that the objectives for which they are accountable would be met. This nonetheless represents a strong constraint on the free play of decentralised decision-making and an inappropriate response to the problem of certainty regarding the overall environmental performance, which could be advantageously resolved through an adequate system of emissions monitoring.

A Regime Based on Prior Authorisation of Each Transaction

Initial experiments with TPs, apart from the programme to phase out leaded petrol in the United States, have generally provided for the planned trading operations to be duly authorised on a case-by-case basis before it can proceed. This procedure is understandable in cases where the emissions or abstractions in question are likely to have significantly different impacts on the environment according to the location of the sources taking part in the trading and where it is important to avoid any hot spot concentrating pollutants or resource abstractions. Other rules (zoning, offset rates) could be used to address this problem in a more satisfactory manner, however, given that the prior authorisation procedure adds considerably to transaction costs (costs of preparing applications; procedural delays that can last for several months; uncertainty about possible social and political interference) and casts serious doubt on whether the transfers envisaged will ever actually take place. For example, during the many months that it takes to complete the procedure, the various parties opposed to the transfers may lobby the authorities and the latter may be influenced by their arguments. All of these are factors that may dissuade economic agents from undertaking transaction, even if they are advantageous from an economic standpoint.

Introduction of Various Restrictions on the Scope for Trading

The strong distrust of permit trading systems that is often apparent in members of the environmental administration and environmental NGOs has in several instances prompted the authorities to introduce various restrictions on trading possibilities. For example, in the case of the Fox river mentioned earlier, transactions which were aimed solely at cutting costs were prohibited; solely those which were aimed at remedying a technological inability to meet standards were allowed to be taken into account (Smith, 1999); and lastly, not a single transaction took place under the programme! Various types of restriction have been tried out in this way:

- *Restrictions on the grounds for trading*, as in the case of the Fox river; needless to say, such restrictions run completely counter to the reasons for which economists originally proposed the introduction of TPs;
- *Spatial restrictions with regard to the territorial boundaries of the trading area*; this type of restriction is the one encountered most frequently and is justified on the grounds of the type of environmental problem considered and the difficulty of finding satisfactory equivalences between different emission sites;
- *Temporal restrictions*; there are two main types of temporal restriction: (a) specification of a period of validity for the permits allocated, for example three months or a year; (b) restrictions or even a ban on TP transfers from one period to another, as in the case of borrowing between periods, which is quite widespread, or less frequently bans on the banking of permits;
- *Restrictions on trading partners*; under some programmes, existing installations are allowed to sell but not to buy permits; only new installations are entitled and indeed obliged to buy the permits needed to cover their emissions. There may also be sectoral restrictions in the case of programmes reserved for a given sector of activities;
- *Restrictions on trade flows*; such restrictions are applied when only one part of the permits held (i.e. a percentage of initial allocation) can be traded.

By their nature, restrictions on trading possibilities, whether or not there are good grounds for such restrictions, have the effect of limiting the number or scale of trades, that is to say the cost savings that are to be expected from this instrument. For example, making permits valid solely for short periods of time, prohibiting transfers from one time period to another and adding spatial restrictions to temporal restrictions will leave very little scope for transfers.

Possibility of Negative Interactions Between the Performance of Transactions and the Administrative Regime Applicable to Permits

A second trade-off must be made between two conflicting objectives, namely providing the necessary legal security to economic agents receiving TPs and preserving the public authorities' ability to revise policy objectives or certain rules of the game in response to external changes or emerging trends such as the deeper awareness of environmental problems among the population, better scientific understanding of the problems in question, experience with the success or failure of the policies pursued, learning how the new instrument functions. These two objectives call for diametrically opposed solutions. Enhancing the legal security of those holding permits leads to greater institutional rigidity which limits the ability of the public authorities to modify their policy other than to impute the cost to public budgets in the form of permit buy-backs by the authorities, which would be contrary to the polluter-pays principle as defined by the OECD in 1972[6]. On the other hand, attempts by government to preserve its room for manoeuvre increases the institutional risk for decentralised agents and discourages them from playing the game of permit trading.

From this point of view, changing the rules of the game relating to a programme is a critical operation. What form of predictability or security can the authorities offer regulated agents with regard to the conditions under which changes will be made? Uncertainty over this question can act as a powerful brake on transfers, as shown by the low use of banking options during the first stage of experimentation with TPs in the United States (Hahn and Hester, 1989*a* and *b*). When making transactions economic agents indirectly disclose information regarding the scope they have for reducing pollutant emissions. If the rule for the allocation of future permits is not defined *ex ante* or if it can be amended at the discretion of the administrative supervising body, a potential vendor might rightly fear that the allocation to which he would be entitled in the future might be adversely affected by his transactions, in which case he might refrain from carrying them out. The risk of bias in transfer operations is even greater if the programme is designed to extend over several periods with the rules being revised at each stage; if the programme is limited to a single period, on the other hand, there is no danger of such interference.

In order to overcome the risk of distrust on the part of agents, it is therefore important to specify beforehand at what intervals the rules will be revised and to clearly explain the procedures and criteria that will be apply to such revisions.

Uncertainty over the Value of Permits in Practice

Another source of legal uncertainty can potentially affect the value of permits. The TP system is usually added on to other regulatory provisions, for example local health regulations. Indeed, this is one means of solving the problems posed by a uniform system of TPs when the damage arising from deposits is differentiated in territorial terms. The acquisition of permits does not dispense with the requirement to meet other obligations, the number of which will reflect the degree to which the responsibilities of the administration with regard to environmental protection are sub-divided between different territorial levels of political organisation and between different agencies. Furthermore, these other obligations may also be modified over time by the authorities and thus may interfere with the value of permits in practice. Lastly, administrative authorisations, of which TPs often take the legal status provide no protection against challenges to civil liability for injury to persons and damage to goods that might result directly from the pollution emitted by an identified source. In view of these considerations, a given source might be reluctant to acquire permits whose exact value in terms of emission capacity might be uncertain and might be contested by various parties, particularly if such permits were to be held in reserve for future use. It is clearly not always possible to avoid interference between different rules that have different objectives.

The Challenges of Combinatory Compatibility

As simply one of many instruments from which decision-makers can choose, TPs are primarily in competition with other policy instruments to regulate environmental problems. It is possible, however, to seek to combine them with other instruments in order to benefit from certain synergies.

In the case of problems which have already prompted action by the authorities, the competition is asymmetrical in the sense that TPs usually represent no more than a virtual instrument with regard to a given instrument already in place, of which all participants have practical experience. The instruments under discussion therefore cannot be assessed on the same basis. Even if the theoretical superiority of TPs over an existing instrument could be demonstrated according to a given criterion such as economic efficiency, income distribution or the certainty of environmental performance, this would in most cases not be sufficient to warrant a change of instrument if the one already in place yields results deemed to be satisfactory by the main actors involved in the policy-making process. For example, a number of proposals were put forward in Norway with a view to introducing TPs to regulate emissions of SO_2 and subsequently CO_2. These proposals have so far failed to progress further due to the existence of taxes which have already been introduced on the same basis and which in the eyes of the authorities have the major merit of generating tax revenues for the public budget, whereas the advocates of TPs in Norway were very interested in the prospect of permits being issued free of charge (Schreiner, 1998; Høibye, 1999)[7].

The outlook for the development of TPs therefore varies substantially according to whether the aim is to provide a solution to a new problem or to improve existing systems for problems that have already been taken into account. In the former case, it is conceivable that it would be possible to formally place all instruments on an equal footing in order to choose the one that is most appropriate. In the latter case, TPs suffer *a priori* from a crowding-out effect which reduces the chances of their being adopted. In the latter case they must therefore be approached not as an alternative to the instruments in place but as an extension or complement to such instruments.

This seam of complementarity running through various instruments is not solely the result of an approach to transition or adaptation to a given regulatory regime, which would suggest a gradual but comprehensive shift towards a full TP type approach, but may also be characteristic of the best permanent solution to the problems posed in that, for various reasons, combining different instruments can, under certain circumstances, provide a better response to the objectives pursued than the deployment of only one of those instruments.

The advantages to be gained from such a combined approach may firstly be seen in terms of the quality of the environment in cases where no single instrument alone can directly meet the target that has been set, as is perhaps the case with urban pollution (Smith, 1999). In such cases it is through a mix of regulations or voluntary agreements to reduce unit vehicle consumption, to which can be added TP systems (averaging schemes), as in the case of the United States, fuel taxes, urban tolls and parking fees, a diversified supply of transport offering an alternative to private car use, as well as further measures, that it is possible to attempt to address a particularly complex problem.

The gains described above can also be looked for on the economic field, with the view to minimise the costs of achieving a given environmental objective. There are therefore circumstances under which it might be advantageous to combine taxes with TPs, as noted in Chapter 2, page 47.

In other cases where the types of agent required to enter into a commitment to reduce emissions are highly heterogeneous, it is possible to use separate instruments for each individual target group given that the rationale governing their behaviour will reflect the fact that they are not all sensitive to the same variables in their own individual context (price-sensitivity varies from one sector to another according to the competitive structure in each sector). In a population made up of a large number of agents who are all small sources of emissions, the use of a system of TPs might perhaps be unwise[8]. A mix of taxes and minimum standards on consumer products might offer a better solution, leaving TPs for firms of a certain minimum size. The use of different instruments for different target groups poses the general problem of the fairness of the burden-sharing. Ideally, equivalences need to be established between instruments so that each target group contributes fairly to the collective effort to curb pollution.

Lastly, mixes of instruments can be justified on distributive grounds. In the United States, for example, the programme to reduce CFC production combined both a quota trading mechanisms and a tax. The purpose of this tax was not to encourage cuts, but was introduced solely because the authorities did not wish to leave the scarcity rent generated by the programme in the hands of industrial groups.

Adopting such an approach towards instruments can nonetheless present a number of risks in terms of the effectiveness of public action. There are principally two such risks:

- The risk of adding substantially to administrative costs if services, monitoring systems and compliance resources need to be duplicated;
- More seriously, the risk of running disparate components together into a single system; this is undoubtedly the greatest risk for TPs which might lose their appeal on efficiency ground as a result of interference from other instruments designed to meet different objectives.

The benefits and risks must therefore be carefully weighed in each individual case according to the priorities of the programme.

Issues Relating to Distributive Aspects

From Theoretical Possibilities to the Political Economy of Decision-Making

In theory, the use of a given economic instrument should not prejudge the sharing of property rights between the State and civil society or between the different social groups. From a technical point of view, every instrument is *a priori* compatible with a wide variety of distributive solutions. The same cannot be said, however, of the political economy of these instruments, which leads the design of each instrument towards contrasting distributive directions. There are, in fact, two more fundamental questions which lie behind the debate over the choice of instruments (TPs, taxes, regulations or voluntary agreements). The first regards the funding of public expenditure and social security; the second concerns the implicit sharing of property rights to the environment between the community, represented by the State, and the firms responsible for discharging pollutants or extracting resources.

The standard textbook approach based on incentive taxes makes the polluter pay a tax even when the residual pollution he causes is optimal for society, whereas under a regulatory approach the same polluter only bears the cost of compliance with regulations. The implicit distribution of environmental rights in the two cases is clearly different, even if these two approaches are compatible with the polluter-pays-principle[9]. The implicit assumption on which an incentive tax is based is that the community possesses rights to the environment and that private agents who wish to make use of the environment must pay for those rights[10]. A regime of subsidies implicitly recognises the allocation of environmental rights to polluting firms and the resulting need for the State to compensate them for abandoning such rights. The regulatory approach and systems in which TPs are issued free of charge correspond to an intermediate position which acknowledges, within certain limits, the right of firms to use the environment.

The usual case is that the tax generates fiscal resources which the public authorities can put towards the budget either to finance new public expenditure or to replace existing fiscal sources that might have certain disadvantages (OECD, 1997). Technically, the authorities nonetheless have the option of not making use of this potential source of income and of remitting to the polluter community, in accordance with a neutral criterion for redistribution, the resources collected from the latter. In such cases, the use of a tax does not imply a transfer of resources from firms, taken as a whole, to the State.

In the case of TPs, it is a well-known fact that their success in political terms in those countries which have gained a practical experience of their implementation, principally the United States, is largely due to the fact that the initial allocation of permits to polluting firms was made free of charge, although this was not out of any logical or economic necessity (see Chapter 2, page 33). Firms would therefore seem to be the first to benefit from the introduction of TPs, but not other instruments, in the event of a free initial allocation of permits.

For the initial distribution of rights, it would be perfectly feasible, as noted above, to contemplate selling permits either at set prices, which would be comparable to a tax, or through an auction. As in the case of taxation, the sale of permits would lend a fiscal and not merely incentive character to the instrument by generating new public resources. The transfer thus obtained would make it possible to capture rents that would otherwise be appropriated by firms. The counterpart to this would obviously take the form of less profits for polluting firms, even though the instrument would lower the overall costs of environmental policy.

The technique of selling permits at auction is compatible with a wide range of distributive schemes in that it is possible to remit to firms taking part in an auction all or part of the income from the sale of permits in accordance with the "zero-revenue auction" advocated by Hahn and Noll (1982). The return must therefore be based on a criterion that will not affect firms' strategies towards permit acquisition, which are logically based on their assessment of the cost of their options for reducing emissions (marginal cost function for pollution abatement).

A clearer idea of the assumptions and procedures applicable is therefore needed in order to gain an insight into the distributive consequences of TPs. One major question in particular relates to the choice of a basis for comparison. In theory there are two such bases:

- The situation prevailing before the introduction of a new environmental policy, which looks quite natural in the case of new problems but which can nonetheless be misleading since it leads to a confusion between two different aspects: (a) the economic impact of introducing new environmental constraints which very often results in higher production costs in the short term;

(b) the distributive effects relating specifically to the choice of certain instruments to implement the policy in question;

- The regulatory regime which would arise if the TP approach were ultimately to be rejected. Depending upon the situation, this comparative reference is provided by taxation or, more frequently, the administrative *command and control* approach.

It is the second approach which will be used in the following part of this section since the purpose of this study is to determine the properties and impacts of TPs and not to study the more general effects of environmental policies.

Nature and Determinants of Distributive Effects

The changes introduced by a new policy instrument can be evaluated from two different standpoints:

- that of the efficiency of the allocation (of efforts to reduce emissions or the use of natural resources), aimed at minimising the costs to community for a given result or at maximising the results obtained for given resources;
- that of the redistribution of income between the agents that make up an economic community.

The first consideration relates to the volume of wealth produced and corresponds to the availability of tradable and non-tradable services and goods; the second to transfers of given wealth between agents. This is an analytical distinction in that in practice most changes encompass both facets, as illustrated in Figure 5 which shows that the impact of a policy instrument can combine two basic movements, namely progress towards efficiency, in the form of lower total costs for all agents, and a redistribution of income between different categories of agent.

There are five main determinants of the distributive impact of TPs: the rule for initial allocation; the diversification of the options for action open to decentralised agents; the geographical redistribution of pollution; the structure of permit markets (perfect or imperfect competition); and the structure of product markets (price-elasticities of demand).

Rule for Initial Allocation

The rule for the initial allocation of permits has a major impact on the distributive effect of the instrument. The greatest contrast is provided by free distribution and the auctioning technique, as discussed in Chapter 2, page 33 and Chapter 3, page 56. Due to the fact that permits can be traded, the initial allocations will be readjusted in order to secure efficiency gains (lower total costs) compared with the costs that would have arisen from a uniform regulatory approach. The rule for initial allocation will therefore help to distribute both the scarcity rent relating to the introduction of the programme and the cost savings arising from operation of the instrument. The procedures depend upon the impact of economic mechanisms on the permit market and product markets. If local competition is held to be competition between agents subject to the same TP system, and international competition as competition from agents who are not subject to that system, the table of impacts is as follows.

In a context of local competition that allows the cost of permits to be passed through to the price of goods, the free distribution of permits allocates both the scarcity rent and the cost savings to pollutant-emitting firms. By generating an opportunity cost with regard to the use of permits, the scarcity rent tends to drive product prices up while cost savings drive them down, as shown in Figure 6.

When producers are exposed to international competition, they have no possibility of passing on the direct and opportunity costs of emission reductions through the price of their products since product prices are set on the international market. The only possibility they have is of adjusting supply. Depending on the relative weight of cost savings and the opportunity cost of using emission permits, supply will either increase or contract compared with the initial equilibrium resulting from a standard

Figure 5. **Allocative and Distributive Effects in a Trading Economy**

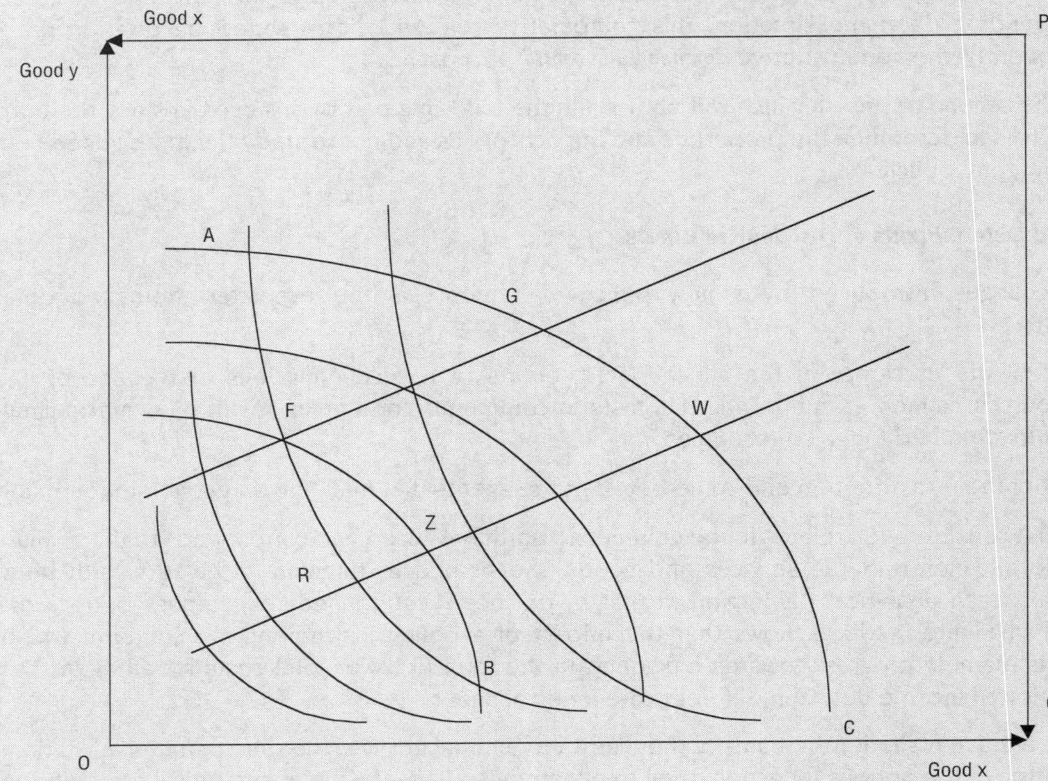

Two agents, O and P, are competing in demand for two goods **x** and **y**. In the figure, the convex curves in relation to their respective origins of O and P represent the indifference curves of each agent in the way in which the two goods, of which fixed total quantities are available, are combined in differing quantities. Thus the curve **AB** corresponds to a set of equivalent combinations for O, and curve **AC** to a set of equivalent combinations for P. Each point on the surface represents a full allocation of goods between the two agents.

The allocative effect centred on economic efficiency corresponds to a change in the distribution of goods that does not lower the utility level of a single agent and that improves the level of utility reached by at least one of them. A distributive effect appears when the improvement to the utility of one of the agents is offset by a decrease in the utility of the other. Moving from point **A** to point **Z** corresponds to a general improvement in the allocation of goods since it is of benefit to both agents who each have access to a higher level of utility than that provided by **A** (from **R** to **Z** for agent O, and from **W** to **Z** for agent P). The **RZW** axis represents efficient allocation. In contrast, moving from **R** to **W** or from **F** to **G** corresponds to a pure distributive effect. From **R** to **W** the movement remains compatible with an efficient allocation; from **F** to **G** the transfer moves the agent from one inefficient state to another inefficient state. Moving from **C** to **R** combines an improvement in efficiency and a redistribution in favour of agent P.

regulatory approach. In both cases, firms' profits will rise due to cost savings, and more so if the opportunity cost is low rather than high since the increase in production will lead to a substantial loss of income from the sale of permits or expensive purchases of permits.

Thus, to a greater or lesser extent depending upon the initial assumptions, the free distribution of permits to firms emitting pollutants results in a transfer from consumers to shareholders, compared with the share-out resulting from a standard regulatory approach. If firms are capable of appropriating the gains in economic efficiency, their cost-competitiveness should be better than under the reference scenario of use of a regulatory instrument, even if it is lower as a result of the introduction of the environmental policy considered. In the case of the Acid Rain Program, it was decided to utilise the free distribution option, the reason being that because the programme targeted services, namely electricity production and distribution, which had been let under a concession to regulated local monopolies, *ad hoc* provisions made by State regulatory commissions were able to force producers to pass on the gains

Figure 6. Distributive Effects of TPs at the Level of Local Competition

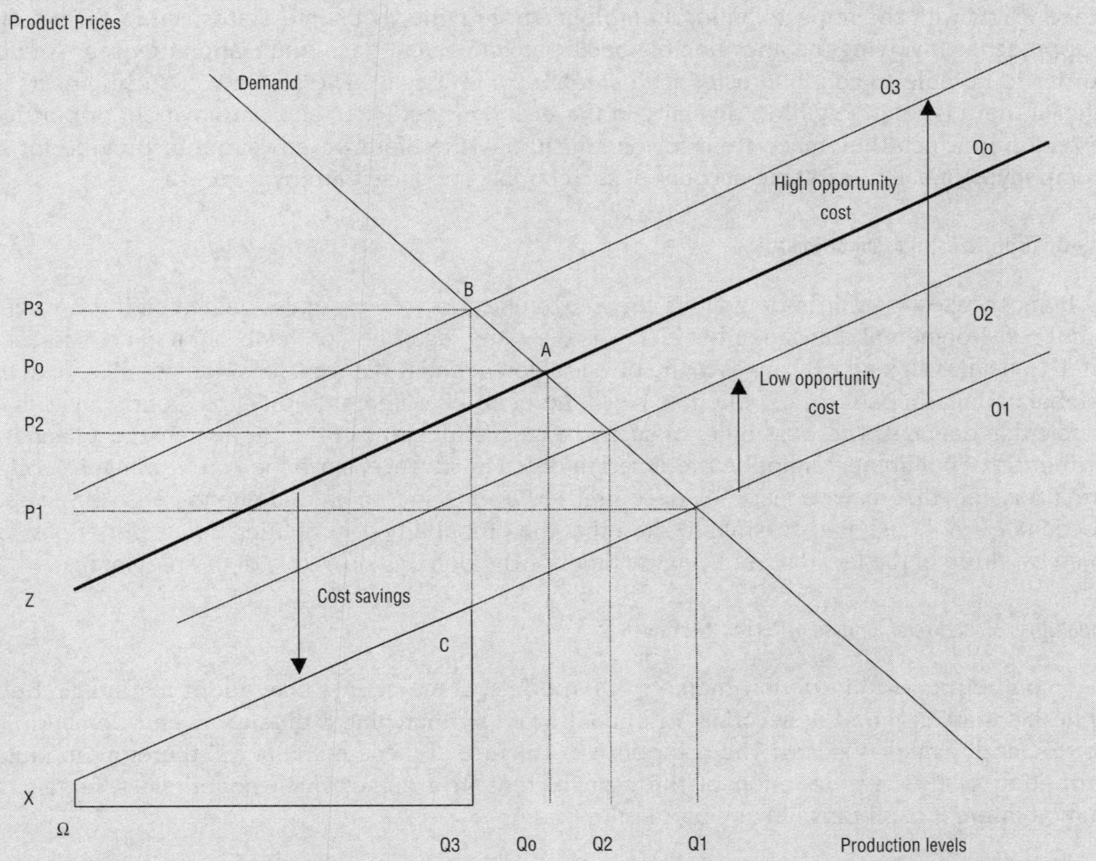

after Harrison, 1994, p. 80

In this Figure, the supply curve Oo corresponds to the costs imposed under a regulatory approach that is relatively inefficient in cost terms. Curve O_1 represents supply incorporating the cost reduction afforded by the use of TPs. Curves O_2 and O_3 represent the supply curves that take account of the opportunity cost to a firm of using the permits itself, since permits have a market value corresponding to the collective marginal cost of avoiding the emission of a unit of pollutant. The ability of a firm to benefit from the corresponding scarcity rent depends on the scope it has for passing on the opportunity costs of using permits to product prices, which will depend upon the price elasticity for the products.

If the opportunity cost is high, the introduction of TPs may shift equilibrium A (Po, Qo) towards equilibrium B (P_3, Q_3). In this case, consumers pay more for products and reduce their demand (from Qo to Q_3). At the same time, the producer's profits rise substantially, since he moves out of the area APoZ into the area BP_3XC. In this particular case, a permit auction would make it more or less possible for this rent to be recovered by the State and redistributed to other agents.

If the opportunity cost is low, which would mean that on the whole the environmental constraint is not particularly severe, the sharp reduction in costs would produce an equilibrium (P_2, Q_2) in which prices would be lower, with the result that both consumers and producers would share the gains arising from the TP system. For this to be a likely outcome, this scenario would require a small number of agents to be exposed to very high abatement costs while the majority of agents would be in a position to abate their emissions at a low cost.

associated with permit trading to consumers through a reduction in tariffs. The same distributive guarantees may not necessarily exist in all cases, however.

Impact of the Diversification of Options for Action Open to Agents

Not only do TPs allow permits to be traded, they also, above all, widen the range of options open to each economic agent, unlike the mandatory use of certain technologies or prescriptive and uniform emissions standards. This diversification may in particular encourage changes in the supply of raw materials in the form of substitutions. This proved to be the case with the Acid Rain Program where low-sulphur content coal produced in the West of the country replaced a high-sulphur content coal produced in the Middle West. Such a substitution is likely to have a significant impact on employment. Indeed it was with the impacts on local employment in mind that some States stated their preference for approaches involving the adoption of specific technologies (desulphurisation devices – scrubbers – in order to be able to continue using high-sulphur content coal). The severity of such impacts may be higher if there is relatively little diversity in the economic activities and employment opportunities in the region in which they make themselves felt. It may therefore be advisable to provide for specific accompanying measures to take account of such impacts on local employment.

Geographical Redistribution of Pollution

In most cases, permit trading alters the geographical pattern of emissions. Even if the value of the residual environmental damage or health risk is the same regardless of the location of the source, certain permit transfers will lead to changes in the physical flow of emissions from local sources. Except in the case of global or uniform patterns of pollution, it will therefore be different population groups who will have to support this damage. The possibility of such changes is inherent in the TP instrument. Changes in the distribution of pollutants cannot be predicted in detail in advance, since they are contingent both on the permit transfers that may be made by decentralised agents and on natural phenomena (wind speed and direction), even though it is possible to show that the probability of benefiting from a better environment is high by virtue of the fact that reducing pollution is the defining objective of the programme.

Competitive Structure of Emission Permit Markets

If competition within permit markets is imperfect, some agents may adopt a strategic behaviour within this market aimed at securing additional profit by matching their supply and demand in a way that will modify market prices. The competitive structure of these markets will therefore modulate the distribution of the appropriation of the scarcity rent in a game which nonetheless remains in the common interest of all those taking part in the trading.

Structure of Product Markets

This variable integrates three types of effect, namely: the origin of the competition, i.e. whether it is local or international; the nature of the competition, i.e. whether or not it permits the strategic use of prices by the firms concerned; the degree of rigidity or flexibility of demand, as determined by price-elasticities. Different mixes produce differing impacts. Faced with international competition that precludes the adjustment of product prices, the auctioning procedure will therefore produce a transfer that will depend upon the use made of the new fiscal resource. If it is used to reduce income tax, the transfers will be away from shareholders and employees towards tax-payers, while the position of consumers remains the same. If it is used to lower employer's contributions, the transfer will be partly towards shareholders and partly towards employees, etc. In response to imperfect local competition and rigid demand, firms can raise their prices; the free distribution of permits would allow them to appropriate both the scarcity rent and the gains arising from trading.

Possible Compensation

TPs make it possible to partially separate two thorny issues: (a) determination of the responsibilities and obligations incumbent on the various agents; (b) the most economical allocation (i.e. which minimises total costs) of emission reduction efforts. Even if the initial distribution of permits is designed solely to meet the criteria of equitable distribution, whatever they may be, the inefficiencies of this allocation could be remedied through the trading mechanism, provided that the transaction costs remain low and that agents cannot derive a strategic advantage from either holding onto or trading in permits (market power).

In the case of an administrative distribution, the possibility of separating these two issues may lead to the rules for permit allocation being viewed as a means of attenuating or compensating for some of the disadvantages and costs of introducing the environmental policy, for example as a means of ensuring that firms exposed to international competition suffer no subsequent dramatic loss of profitability. The distribution of permits going beyond the sole criterion of equal sharing of a given environmental constraint, measured, for example, by a rate of emissions reduction tied to a reference date, might then be seen as a public aid to the firms benefiting from that distribution. If these extra permits are deducted from an overall quota that remains unchanged, then the approach consists of a transfer between firms that are not exposed to international competition and firms that are, since the former will see their allocation decrease in proportion to the increase in that of the latter. In contrast, if these extra permits are added to the ceiling originally agreed, this would be a retrograde move with regard to the environment.

In the event of transaction costs or imperfect competition, the initial rule for allocation will also interfere with the operation of the permit market and may prevent the economically efficient distribution of permits; however, it could be used judiciously to soften the adverse impact of market power, for example, by allocating more permits to small firms than to firms able to make their weight felt on the market.

By and large, if the transaction costs and market imperfections are not negligible, it may be preferable to consider providing other forms of compensation for firms rather than the manipulation of permit distribution procedures. On the other hand, the organisation of TPs may prove invaluable as a means of redistributing scarcity rents widely and fairly, as in the real estate sector. The final choice will depend upon the weightings assigned respectively to the allocative and distributive objectives.

Furthermore, it needs to be realised that the economic gains afforded by TPs will not be sufficient to offset any unfair or unacceptable aspects of the initial allocation; those who may lose out in the initial allocation will continue to lose out, even if they lose less because they can trade permits than they would have were they unable to.

Issues Relating to Social Impacts and Political Acceptability

The use of economic instruments to implement environmental policy has in the past been viewed with considerable scepticism and these doubts have yet to be fully allayed. There are several reasons for such misgivings. One reason is the asymmetry in perceptions in that the costs imposed by economic instruments (TPs, environmental taxes) are readily identifiable, whereas the costs of a regulatory approach are far less easy to discern and cannot be expressed spontaneously in the form of aggregate, synthetic and popular figures, even if the overall total is significantly higher due to the inefficiencies it generates. Mistrust of the way in which public institutions operate, when it exists, also includes instruments whose attributes and use might subsequently be redirected at the discretion of public authorities or administrative services. Tax-related issues are generally highly sensitive, raising great fears that accepting a new tax will pave the way to huge excesses in the future. Mention should also be made of the general ignorance of how these economic instruments actually work. Attention is often focused exclusively on the financial and distributive aspects of such instruments, while their role as incentives is almost universally disregarded.

There can be little doubt that political acceptability is still the weak point of TPs in most of the world's countries – often, it must be said, for the wrong reasons. In addition to the more general reasons for agents' misgivings there is also the concern over the conflict between the field of action (environmental protection and natural resources management) and certain attributes of the instrument, primarily the idea of a "right to pollute" and that of the right to sell such rights to pollute. In addition to these basic objections to the legitimacy of the instrument there are also more circumstantial factors such as the fears of local populations, with regard to both the environment and the potential impact on local employment, and resistance on the part of agents who lose some of their discretionary powers were a TP system to be introduced.

Box 15. **Distribution of Additional Permits to Secure Approval for a TP Programme**

In several cases (the Acid Rain Program in the United States, fisheries regulation in New Zealand, the RECLAIM programme in California), the political authorities issued more than the number of permits they had originally decided would be the maximum from an environmental standpoint simply to ensure that the reform would be acceptable to the parties concerned. Admittedly, the distribution of additional permits was accompanied by *ad hoc* measures designed to limit the scope of such permits to a transitional period: for the Acid Rain Program, for example, these extra permits were restricted to the first years of the first period 1995 to 1999; for the RECLAIM programme they were non-transferable and restricted to the first years; in New Zealand, they were accompanied by a permit buy-back programme put in place by the authorities for a total of 16 000 tonnes of fish landed (Wallis, 1999).

These misgivings and difficulties are in large part attributable to a general lack of understanding of the issues relating to TPs and the nature of such permits, which would seem to suggest that the prospects for future development of this instrument are promising provided that its promoters are willing to make the necessary investment beforehand to share with the highest possible number of agents the reasons for which they favour this instrument and the knowledge they have of how it works. The problem of social acceptability must not be taken lightly. Issuing permits free of charge will not alone be sufficient to overcome a multiform opposition (see Box 15).

On the "Right to Pollute"

An economist will say that the environment consists of a set of collective goods susceptible to overloading, thus of goods which if made subject to unregulated private management would easily be overexploited and wasted. A lawyer will say that the most essential components of the environment, and air in particular, cannot be appropriated by reason of their physical characteristics and, as things which must remain accessible to each and everyone, have the status of *res communis* under civil law (Rémond-Gouilloud, 1989)[11]. Use of a common good is limited by the requirement that use should not be detrimental to other users of the same good. The obligations involved are similar to those with private servitudes: the use covered by the servitude must not result in loss of the good's substance.

On this point there would seem to be a radical antagonism between what the environment means for present-day society, and in particular for environmentalists (the environment must be accessible to all and must not be appropriated by anyone), and the very nature of TPs. Strict application of *res communis* rules would mean a ban on industrial waste or motor vehicles if they caused damage for other users. But since the beginning of the industrial age positive law has tolerated the reverse, on the grounds of the greater benefits that industrial development would bring the community. Environmental policies set in hand over the past 20 or 30 years are seeking to pull back that tolerance over the long term, as is shown for instance by the objectives agreed in the Geneva Convention on long-range atmospheric pollution. The aim of that Convention is to reduce acid deposition to below the level at which damage might be detected. In the eyes of some of the protagonists in environmental policy-making, the aim of sustainable development can mean nothing else, although this view is quite disputable.

But that cannot be achieved in the short run. Policymakers steering the transition accordingly have to find the most economically efficient implementing instruments to ensure that the final objective will remain acceptable to the parties who will be called upon to bear the costs. This is where TPs come in: as an economic tool for trade-offs among different uses of the environment, which all help to degrade the *res communis*, by accepting some of them in a limited and temporary manner with increasingly stringent rationing over time. TPs can fit a long term aim of preserving the substance of the *res communis* and safeguarding access for all users who do not damage it.

Rationing some harmful uses can help preserve a *res communis*. Once rationing is in place, the TP mechanism can come into play to spread and share in a flexible way the constraint without breaching the protective aims. In this way, neither the air nor the environment are appropriated but instead a number of harmful uses are restricted and the scope for trading permits is designed to secure the most economically effective allocation of rationing. Against this background, the provocative expression "right to pollute", which is sometimes unwisely used in the literature with reference to emission permits, is particularly misplaced as the aim of TPs is not to recognise a new right to harm where no such right existed before, but to severely restrict the exercise of this right in areas where it was unlimited or already recognised in the regulations. The concept of rights has a positive connotation in the context of basic rights, whereas, if taken literally, the concept of a "right to pollute" is perceived as a cynical and negative notion that establishes a right to harm others.

On the Right to Sell a "Right to Pollute"

Some social groups and non-governmental organisations argue that pollution is not only the use of natural resources or collective goods in a way that leads to over-exploitation, but an inherently reprehensible act, a moral evil, in that an attack is made upon the right of others to live in healthy environment, both in an aesthetic sense and in terms of physical well-being, or upon nature itself. Those who hold this view recognise that it might admittedly be a necessary evil in an industrial civilisation that has reached a given stage of development, but consider that this evil needs to be allayed as much as possible by means of technology. From this standpoint, a public reward cannot be given to those who do no more than reducing the evil they cause or, worse still, such persons cannot be allowed to earn money by selling a "right to pollute" to other unscrupulous firms. Trading in pollutant emission permits would therefore be immoral by nature. Here it is the pecuniary and commercial side to the issue that is held to be immoral, whereas economists see TPs as an effective means of making transfers that are of benefit to all parties. In contrast, the idea of a non-commercial transfer of permits between different agents does not in itself appear to pose any problems in terms of acceptability.

The Controversy over Acquired Rights

Even if the above issues can be resolved, the political decision still remains as to how rights to the environment are to be shared out between different interest groups and what course of action should be taken with regard to any rights acquired previously by economic agents whose polluting activities

Box 16. **The Controversy over Acquired Rights**

Depending upon one's point of view, the same procedure for introducing TPs may be perceived as either the attribution of new rents or an increase in the costs associated with a given activity. It all depends on the implicit reference situation which actors use to form an opinion. Those who perceive primarily the TP system as the introduction of new constraints necessitating new expenditures base their opinion on a situation in which the constraints were either lower or non-existent and in which they had more rights (to abstract or emit), without having to pay for access. Those who see in the initial allocation of permits the distribution of a new form of valuable assets only consider the fact that here value results from a type of scarcity that is the outcome of the collective actions and choices taken by society and not from the labour or individual merit of the agents. Once it is accepted that permits can be transferred through a commercial transaction, they must be viewed in the same light as any other public allocation of assets.

The disagreement is fundamentally over the existence of rights acquired under the previous regulatory regime. The approach adopted by permit users is to defend the idea that the new policy challenges the economic context in which they invested in a given activity and that there is therefore a breach of the moral contract they had entered into with the public authorities. Other agents take the opposite view that the administrative authorisations issued in the past conferred no definitive right that can be upheld against change in the policy of the public authorities, who have the power, if it is felt to be of public necessity, to modify the regulatory regime.

have been duly authorised in the past by the public authorities. There are conflicting perceptions of the rules of permit allocation to enterprises that release pollutants. Defended by business, free allocation is considered illegitimate by numerous NGOs, certain government circles and certain segments of public opinion on the grounds that it is tantamount to a bonus for polluters, or even a wrongful transfer to private parties of parts of the common patrimony by the community. Conflicts between different groups of stakeholders in connection with initial allocation of permits were one of the reasons for the failure of TPs in the United Kingdom (Sorrell, 1999) and explain the rather laborious launch of the Acid Rain and RECLAIM programs in the United States (Harrison, 1999).

The Principle of Non-Transferability of Administrative Authorisations

Administrative law itself poses a number of obstacles which, although serious, are not insuperable. They relate to the principles on which relations between the State and civil society are based. In several countries, including France, one of the basic principles of public law is that administrative authorisations cannot be transferred to another party and can certainly not be sold. As emanations or parts of the State's authority and sovereignty, administrative authorisations do not confer any right that can then be upheld against the State or transferred to other economic agents via a monetary transaction: in no event does the recipient of an authorisation become its owner; in that case, he cannot dispose of it and, in particular, to transfer it[12]. Regulatory requirements on pollution are widely implemented via administrative authorisations to conduct the polluting activity, however, and TPs are usually accorded the same status.

To overcome this obstacle, the most direct solution, technically speaking, would no doubt be to convert the status of the legal instrument employed, by replacing administrative authorisations with property rights. But that would be tantamount to granting on a permanent basis user rights to collective goods which by statute, as in France, are the common assets of the nation. There is a major political incompatibility here which has been observed in all countries where TPs have been tried out, most particularly in the United States.

The United States authorities have declined to give up their discretionary powers to decide which policy objectives to pursue, and hence to take the compensation road to further progress in combating pollution. That is why, even in the United States, TPs are administrative authorisations and not property rights (Godard, 1994). But the statutory security of economic agents has been safeguarded in the Acid Rain Program by setting out the terms on which permits are allocated to power stations in the Federal Act adopted by the Congress itself, and guaranteeing power plants operated before the beginning of the programme a pre-set annual allocation for thirty years. The Environmental Protection Agency has no scope, in law, to alter those allocation rules. But a vote by Congress could amend the status of TPs already allocated, without the need to compensate holders.

Fears of the Local Population

The possibility of transferring permits between economic agents or from one source to another swiftly aroused the fears of local populations which saw such schemes as a threat either to the quality of their environment or to the prospects for local employment.

With TPs, no local community would be immune from new exposure to pollution and it would not have at its disposal the means of controlling this new exposure directly at source, which would depend solely upon a decision taken freely by the two industrial partners to a transaction. This is a problem of asymmetrical distribution of benefits and costs. The economic gains from TPs would primarily benefit firms and, in certain situations, consumers who might benefit from lower product prices; these beneficiaries are agents dispersed geographically throughout and outside (for consumers) the entire area within which TPs apply. In terms of damage to the environment, the prospect of transactions being made creates a moral risk that each local population might see damage to its environment as a result of transactions, even if it can expect to have a symmetrical chance of seeing its environment improve for the same reasons. However, agents do not all place the same value on the risk of a loss and chance of a gain (Tversky and Kahneman, 1981), hence the concern of all local populations, even though overall the TP programme is based on the reduction of emissions which can but improve the overall environmental situation.

Fears over the prospects for local employment tend to focus on several parameters in a TP programme:

- Whether or not a charge will be levied on initial quota allocations, given that the financial impact of charging for permits may prompt firms to close certain facilities (see the discussion of this point in Chapter 3, page 56);
- In the event of a free allocation, the size of quotas and, by corollary, the level of effort required;
- Whether or not there are prior authorisation procedures that would provide a safeguard against transfers that would have a negative social impact;
- The rules to apply in the event of a drastic reduction in the activity covered by permits or the cessation of such activity; recognition of the scope for firms to retain control over permits that it ceases to use due to the closure of an establishment is generally vigorously opposed in that it is perceived by labour organisations as a direct incentive to close facilities in order to invest elsewhere to the detriment of the local economy and local employment.

This concern over employment must be taken into account on a case-by-case basis and may require the introduction of specific support measures, notably in the form of vocational training, in cases where the entry into force of the programme has to be accompanied by industrial reconversion. These measures must nonetheless be designed not to undermine the economic properties that make TPs attractive since it is by allowing the costs of an environmental programme to be kept as low as possible that any adverse impacts on the local economy and employment can be reduced.

The Fear of a Loss of Market Power on the Part of Different Actors

The introduction of economic instruments significantly alters the respective roles of the actors involved in pollution management or the regulation of resource exploitation in that a decentralised economic mechanism is substituted for the body of administrative procedures within which certain actors can acquire significant discretionary power. This can lead to opposition from the administrations in charge of managing environmental regulations and the technical departments responsible for the environment and industrial safety within firms.

The administrative officials in public services are therefore frequently members of groups hostile to the development of TPs, since introduction of the latter would remove their oversight from the choices of technology made by firms. Similarly, the introduction of TPs can lead to changes in the organisation of internal responsibilities within firms by assigning responsibility for environmental matters to financial, and no longer solely engineering, departments. This shows that the successful introduction of TPs is not simply a matter of technological change in the interests of greater efficiency, it also requires a change in the culture of an organisation which hitherto had been shared by administrative departments and firms on the basis of technical regulations regarding pollution.

The Fear of Compromising Corporate Reputation

Different misgivings and opposition in regard to TPs tend to coalesce to create a climate that is not wholly favourable to the development of TPs in countries that as yet have no practical experience of such programmes. Even when regulatory regimes have been opened up in certain domains, major firms which manage their reputation as a strategic asset (Godard, 1993*b*) are forced to show caution before committing themselves to transactions involving TPs in certain countries, even if such transactions allow them to make significant savings in costs. This would appear to be borne out by the lack of any practical application of the TP schemes introduced in certain Swiss cantons in order to combat air pollution (Jeanrenaud, 1999). Industrial groups that have made sustainable development and environmental protection one of the pillars of their communications strategy may feel that the purchase or sale of emission permits might compromise their credentials as environmentally-friendly firms in the eyes of public opinion.

Choice of Words

In the context that has been outlined above, the names given to TP schemes can assume major symbolic importance in the public debate. The terms currently used are a mix of the categories used by the United States Environmental Protection Agency and the academic language of economists. To address the different instruments of flexibility in terms of "property rights" and "market", and even "market for rights to pollute", may be a good strategy in certain countries and at certain times when these expressions are valued as essential or founding elements of the social system. But in other regions of the world where society's perception of the market and private ownership is much more ambivalent there also has to be some supplementary reference to concepts like citizenship, community and solidarity, as well as free access of persons to nature and the basic amenities of the environment.

Thus a militant market ideology, out of tune with the diversity of actual experience, can make it difficult to develop certain types of practical regulatory arrangements bringing flexibility and generally considered as TPs. It surely cannot be a coincidence that labelling the plan for using TPs to organise reduced consumption and production of CFCs in industrial countries an "industrial rationalisation scheme" was accompanied by a complete lack of public outcry?

Notes

1. From a policy viewpoint, the issue of the legitimacy of this asymmetry has to raised. It is legitimate if it reflects differences in acuity of environmental problems, preferences of people or responsibility in the creation of problems; in that case policy should not seek to counterbalances resulting changes in competition conditions. It is illegitimate if asymmetry only reflects policy failures or a strategic use of environmental policies in favour of some business interests.
2. Due to the sensitivity of public opinion and the vigilance of non-governmental organisations working in the environment sector, many multinational firms seek to safeguard their reputation for environmentally-sensitive management, even if in some cases this may involve their foregoing the opportunity to take advantage of the lower costs available in certain countries whose regulatory regimes are less stringent than those in the most advanced industrial countries.
3. For example, steel is a product that generates a high volume of trade in a highly international market. In contrast, because of the weight of transport costs compared with the value of the product at the factory gate, cement markets are geographically fragmented and the competition assumes specific local forms.
4. In a Cournot duopoly, each firm considers the quantities sold by the other as parameters and uses these to determine a monopoly price for the market segment to which it is entitled.
5. For an analysis of the French case to this regard, see Cros and Godard (1996) and Cros (1999).
6. The ability to adjust environmental policy to new circumstances without placing a further burden on public finances was one of the reasons for recognition of the polluter-pays principle by the OECD (Godard, 1995*b*). The OECD Council adopted a recommendation regarding the polluter-pays principle (PPP) which states in particular that "The Principle ... means that the polluter should bear the expenses of carrying out the measures ... to ensure that the environment is in an acceptable state" (OECD, 1975).
7. The Norwegian Parliament nonetheless called for a study to be made of the TP system for CO_2.
8. Even for global warming, the most important environmental problem in quantitative terms, administrative and transaction costs may turn down as unrealistic the prospect of an involvement of every citizen in a TP market: in a country like UK or France, the annual allocation that would have to be managed, based on an annual rate of emission of approximately 3 tonnes of carbon per adult and a permit value of $40 in 2010, would amount to $120 per adult, whereas the administrative costs of issuing these permits might well be greater, not to mention the cost of permit trading *per se*: transactions would have to give rise to double accounting, in national currency and carbon, for household expenses on fuel and domestic energy. In France, the government declines to collect income tax in cases where the amount due falls below a certain level which in 1997 was set at 61 euros.
9. As indicated by the definition recalled in Footnote 18, the PPP is therefore not a principle of full internalisation of the external costs of pollution. See OECD (1975).
10. In France, for example, this assumption reflects the Act on Nature Protection of July 1976 which, under Article 1, asserts that the protection of the countryside, animal species and natural resources is in the common interest, and also Article 110 of the Town Planning Code which states that "the territory of France is the common heritage of the nation".
11. This writer takes air as a typical example of resources that defy any appropriation on account of their physical characteristics. Since it cannot be measured and the measurement recorded, it cannot be protected and hence legally owned (Rémond-Gouilloud, 1989, p. 108).
12. It will be noted that, symmetrically, administrative authorisations are granted, with some exceptions, subject to the rights of third parties: although authorised, an activity which harms the goods or persons of other parties is bound under civil law to make reparation.

Chapter 4

Making an Informed Decision to Introduce Transferable Permits

In order to meet specific environmental objectives, policy-makers can avail themselves of a wide range of economic and non-economic instruments. While admittedly they may have certain preferences, not all instruments are equally suited to the different problems to be addressed or to the contexts in which policy-makers might wish to apply them. It is therefore useful to consider the conditions in which the use of TPs would be more adequate than that of other instruments, notably incentive taxes. Such an assessment depends upon the nature of the problem to solve, the existing institutional context and on meeting certain economic conditions.

The Nature of the Problem

TPs are instruments at the service of environmental and natural resource management policies. They are not an end in themselves. The first constraint that legitimately weighs on their adoption therefore concerns their ability to further the objectives set for those policies by local or national public authorities. The question to be answered is a simple one. Can TPs fit the problem of concern? Looked at from this angle, TPs have two essential features: (a) they prescribe a quantitatively defined obligation or right to be assigned or allocated to local agents within a specified space-time frame; (b) they allow them to transfer all or part of their assigned obligations or allocated rights, both of which having been set in quantitative terms.

Consequently the first prerequisite is so self-evident that it hardly needs to be formulated: for a system of TPs to come into being, the objectives of environmental policy must really "bite" and not be just cosmetic applications to a spontaneous or exogenous economic trend or technological development. If the constraint represented by the objectives is not active, no specific action needs to be initiated and the notion of efficient distribution of effort ceases to be meaningful – in such a case, if TPs were in place, the parties concerned would in fact have no need to make transfers. This was one of the main reasons why the United Kingdom decided not to go on with its programme of transferable quotas designed to combat SO_2 pollution: the massive switch from coal to gas-fired power plants, following privatisation of the electricity sector, completely altered the nature of the problems posed by compliance with the objectives accepted by that country under the Geneva Convention and its implementing protocols (Steedman, 1999; Sorrell, 1999).

In order to analyse situations in which environmental policy objectives take on their own unique characteristics and specific instruments have to be used, there are three fundamental entities that form an environmental problem: a pollution source, a physical system, and a target (a species to be protected, a feature of the system to be preserved). The morphological constraints of adjusting a policy instrument to the objectives derive from these three entities.

Aims and the Target

The greater the extent to which environmental quality objectives can be formulated in aggregated quantitative terms permitting significant space-time equivalencies, the more readily the problem can be addressed by TPs. Conversely, if the environmental constraints have to be scrupulously respected in a very narrow space-time frame, the less scope there will be for the use of TPs. Furthermore, the policy objectives concerned have to be quantitative or predictably linked to activities measurable by a limited number of flows. Thus pollutant emissions must be apprehended through a limited number of basic categories such as SO_2, NO_x, volatile organic compounds (VOC), particles. In the case of natural resources the categories will consist of cubic metre abstractions of water or tonnage catches of fish of different species. Or they have to relate to standardised or fundamental activities involving different agents such as building rights determined by density ratios, fishing rights in terms of days of activity for a given type of vessel, as in New Zealand, Iceland and the Netherlands.

In a given environment, obviously the physical characteristics of the target have to be taken into account. If it is sought to preserve certain features of the landscape, such as verges and hedgerows in rural areas or architecture compatible with the history of human settlement, it is hard to see how TPs can be applied to these objectives. It is different with objectives as to building density in certain urban and peri-urban areas. Then there is a good case for an arrangement that combines allocation of transferable building rights to all local landowners with a zoning plan specifying density ceilings and, by implication, the amount of rights to be accumulated in order to be able to build in this or that zone. Under this type of arrangement, property developers have to purchase the requisite rights from those holding them, hence a wider distribution of the scarcity rent accruing to building rights as a result of zoning (Renard, 1999) and, theoretically (if all the external effects of building are internalised), the choice of projects that maximise the collective surplus.

A change of target over time may open up new possibilities. For instance, when phosphate and nitrogen discharges reach fairly high levels, they create local pollution problems (e.g. water eutrophication) which are circumscribed by strict space-time constraints that limit the possibility of using TPs. As the rates of dispersion fall, the local problems become less acute and are eventually replaced by problems of non-point pollution, mainly of agricultural origin, the effects of which are produced over longer distances and longer periods as far as the final repositories of these phosphate and nitrogen compounds, such as river estuaries and lakes. When that stage is reached, non-point pollution of agricultural origin can be incorporated along with point pollution in a system of TPs designed to reduce the overall nitrogen and phosphorus load arriving in these repositories. This is what has been attempted in the recent plan for water-quality management of Lake Dillon in Colorado: although bound by a programme of discharge reduction, the point sources may raise their discharges above the prescribed limit if they invest in abatement of non-point pollution of agricultural origin (Kraemer and Banholzer, 1999). Because of uncertainty about the effectiveness of this type of scheme, an offset of 2 to 1 was fixed. Thus, given the same generic type of pollution, a shift of target alters the acceptable equivalencies and hence opens up new possibilities in the choice of instruments.

Characteristics of the **Environment**

The characteristics of the environment may impose specific constraints on the choice of instrument or on the options available in terms of flexibility (see Box 17 on the management of the thermal pollution of rivers).

Thus certain spaces contain ecosystems of special, if not unique, ecological value. It is therefore difficult to allow transfers involving these spaces, since this may lead to authorising a polluting industrial activity in them or shifting the protection device to other spaces: the necessary measurements are too complex (biodiversity indices cannot suffice) and the acceptable equivalencies are lacking.

Even under such apparently unfavourable circumstances, it is possible, by exercising a certain degree of imagination, to seek to complement the usual means of protection by a TP system. This might take the form of a general requirement – for any economic agent wanting to encroach on natural spaces having a definite ecological importance, without being exceptional – to rehabilitate deteriorated natural spaces in other locations over an equivalent surface area. This requirement could be made transferable by authorising the agent concerned to assign its fulfilment, under a business contract, to an agent specialising in rehabilitation. A market for rehabilitation of deteriorated natural spaces could thus be

Box 17. **Thermal Pollution of Rivers**

The thermal pollution of rivers by discharges from power plants must not instantly raise the water temperature above a certain level, this in order to preserve the biological balance of the watercourse and, in particular, so as not to disturb relations between the different fish populations. In this context, it is difficult to authorise arrangements for "banking" or transfer of heat emission rights which might have the effect of bunching thermal discharges in certain periods or on certain sites, regardless of the local damage caused.

On the other hand, in a hypothetical situation where several plants release discharges into the same section of a watercourse, it would be quite possible to have a system whereby each plant had transferable heat emission permits (a maximum discharge of x therms/second). Such a system could well prove economically advantageous if the different plants experienced fluctuations in activity attributable to their production process, their markets or their being part of a plant pool. The same would apply if they had alternative options enabling them to limit their thermal discharges or to release them elsewhere than in the watercourse. The situation here would then resemble the classic case of "bubble" regulation of air pollution in an industrial area.

developed, although it would first be necessary to define categories of deteriorated spaces and formulate standard specifications for rehabilitation with different cost categories. This market would not replace but coexist with non-transferable action to protect natural spaces of exceptional importance.

Source Characteristics

Source characteristics also play a role in determining whether TPs can or should be used. If there is no more than one source in the space-time frame concerned, it is obviously unnecessary to have a system of permit trading. This applies, for example, to sea disposal of radioactive waste from nuclear power stations or reprocessing plants. At the local level there are so few of these facilities that there is no point in organising a trading system.

If there are enough sources to warrant trading, they each must have the means available at the local level to be able to adjust their pollution emissions. When pollution or other environmental damage is the inevitable consequence of a given activity, there may be little advantage to be gained from TPs, in which case the emission or abstraction permits should be replaced by permits to carry out that activity, if these authorisations can be expressed quantitatively. This could apply to fishing rights or, theoretically, rights of access to certain natural spaces, rather in the manner of restricted club membership.

The intrinsic aim of TPs is not to regulate the whole field of environmental policy and the management of natural resources. However, it would nonetheless appear to be feasible to design TP schemes to address problems for which they might not at first sight seem suitable. The scope of application of such an approach extends far beyond air pollution and fisheries management. The conclusion that may be drawn is that the chief technical obstacles to TP application are not primarily attributable to the nature of the problems posed by management of the environment and natural resources, but in:

- the imprecision of policy objectives;
- the difficulty of quantifying the key variables;
- the difficulty of formulating acceptable equivalencies between phenomena (emission, capture, abstraction) occurring at different points in the space-time matrix.

The Existing Institutional Context

Extensive reforms are costly for those who undertake them and for those who bear the consequences. The latter have to contend with the costs of adjustment and learning, new uncertainties and, possibly, permanently higher operating costs. For the policy-makers, the reforms can be costly in terms of time, reputation, new enmities and splits, budget resources, and lowered performance during the period of transition and learning. Reforms are therefore investments, which are made only when the advantages expected by the reformers are sufficient to outweigh these initial costs. This is why institutional innovation is usually phased in through a succession of small changes to the existing set-up, at a pace that allows these changes to be assimilated by the organisations that cause the regulatory system to function. So new provisions are continually added to the existing arrangements, until the whole system becomes so complicated that it is necessary to reintroduce consistency by way of a radical adjustment or overhaul of the legislation.

In the case of TPs, this situation may have one of three outcomes:

- Since the bases for certain environmental policies were historically different to those for TP schemes (other concepts, other procedures, other organisations), it is simply common sense to acknowledge that it would now be far too costly to dismantle the entire existing system to reconstruct a regulatory system better suited to the use of TPs. In particular, if the national styles of environmental policy are based on a combination of regulatory and financial mechanisms, as is the case in Europe, there might not be enough room left for TPs if the authorities hope to avoid an in-depth reform of their regulatory systems.

- The desire to modernise the existing regulatory regime and improve its economic efficiency may argue in favour of adopting a gradual and incremental approach towards the introduction of TPs, provided that the initial conditions provide an acceptable starting point for the type of operation implicit in TP schemes. As well as avoiding the cost of a radical reform, this approach also affords participants an initial opportunity to familiarise themselves with the implications of such an economic instrument.

- In view of the cost of an in-depth reform of existing systems preference might be given to a third approach, namely to restrict the development of TPs to new problems by constructing a new administrative framework *ab initio* designed to operate alongside the existing systems, which would continue to be used to direct public efforts to combat conventional problems; at least it would be possible in this way to put in place a coherent organisational system that is consistent with the principles on which the instrument is based in order to fully exploit its potential; but there must not be too much friction between the new arrangement and the older one, or the expected economic benefits will not materialise; when the same given activity is responsible for the emission of several pollutants, this friction is bound to occur.

TPs can therefore be used to meet type different types of objective, namely either to improve the existing system by providing greater flexibility or to put in place a new system designed to exploit the potential of the instrument to the full. A study of experience with TPs for water management, mainly as regards the allocation of irrigation rights (Kraemer and Banholzer, 1999), shows that successful schemes are those that are rooted in well-established and often very long-standing institutions and governance systems. Even in the case of a new problem, incorporating the new system into a pre-existing regime can be enough to ensure its success, as suggested by US programme to introduce lead-free petrol (Nussbaum, 1992). This does not exclude the success of entirely new systems designed to address problems that had not been dealt with hitherto, such as the Acid Rain Program, and does not guarantee the success of systems that were designed only as extensions to existing regulatory approaches (Harrison, 1999) (see Box 18).

Thus, the greater the degree to which public action has been institutionalised, through wide-ranging legislation and an administrative organisation developed at several territorial levels and channelled

Box 18. **The First Phase of US Experience Prior to 1990**

In this first phase, the new schemes proposed since 1977 were designed to introduce flexibility into the regulatory framework. The chief problem posed was solved, inasmuch as industrial development has not been blocked in the areas unable to comply on time with federal standards of environmental quality (in California principally). On the other hand, only very partial cost savings were obtained. This was because of obstacles created by the regulatory system already in place and by the overly restrictive and bureaucratic rules that were introduced. Furthermore, the baseline situation was still too indeterminate for it to be possible to identify emission credit rights easily and predictably. All told, this procedure by trial and error was instructive and the lessons learned were incorporated into the 1990 CAAA. Would it have been possible to do without this process of experimentation and learning?

Table 4. **Options for the Introduction of Transferable Permits**

Institutional Framework	Problem	
	Already covered	New
Extension of existing framework and/or addition of greater flexibility on the margin	*Examples*: "bubbles" for air pollution from an industrial complex; "averaging" of energy consumption requirements over a range of products	*Example*: Extension of the application of BATs and the IPPC EU directive to the regulation of greenhouse gases, leaving little margin for the use of economic instruments
New and separate programme for TPs and retention of the existing general framework	*Example*: introduction of the Acid Rain Program in the United States in addition to local regulations designed to curb SO_2 emissions	*Example*: Introduction of a separate programme of transferable quotas for carbon emissions not covered by the EU directive on IPPC
General regulatory reform to adjust the institutional framework to the thrust of economic instruments	*Example*: Replacement of a standard regulatory control policy by the RECLAIM programme of TPs in the Los Angeles district	*Example*: General policy of developing TPs in various areas of environmental protection, like the general policy of the EPA in the United States

through several services or agencies, the harder it would seem to be to introduce a new system designed on a different basis. It nonetheless remains possible to modify the boundaries of the existing system in order to improve its efficiency.

The choice of which of the three strategies to adopt depends upon the response that can be made to the question over the existing institutional context: does it provide a suitable basis on which to develop a TP programme? If the answer is no, then either an entirely new and tailor-made system must be put in place specifically to address the problem to be dealt with or the existing system must be completely overhauled in order to adapt it. The attractiveness of these options will depend upon whether the authorities find themselves dealing with an environmental problem that is already covered by the administrative and regulatory framework in place or with a new problem from the standpoint of public policy. The various options open are summarised in Table 4 and illustrated by examples of which some are real and others fictitious.

Favourable Economic Circumstances

Economic analysis does not claim that TPs are a panacea for all situations. There are a number of circumstances in which it may caution against use of this instrument and argue for an approach such as taxation or regulation.

Modest or Insignificant Transaction Costs

In economics literature, transaction costs are a set of costs imposed by a regulatory mechanism (Williamson, 1985): costs of partner search; administrative costs of authorisation procedures; costs of monitoring and of the information needed in order to identify right-holders, tracking of transactions and adjusting the accounts of each transactor; cost of the system of checking compliance of actual performances; cost of initiating proceedings in the event of default; insurance costs. In some cases, these costs can be so high as to cancel out the cost savings allowed by transfers, particularly when the latter take the form of external transactions. This could be the case with TP application to consumption of necessities like retail packaging and energy (fossil fuels) by end users (e.g. motorists, households having to heat their homes). It would also be the case with systems designed for very small geographic areas, with few possible partners and lengthy authorisation and negotiation procedures. Thus it might be wise to focus on specific categories of participants rather than apply the same treatment to all.

The next step, therefore, could be to consider instrument mixes for individual targets and sectors. These mixes could be designed in such a way as to minimise total transaction costs. Industry, for example, could have a system of auctionable permits for its air pollution emissions, while pollution from private transport would be taxable.

Threshold Effects or the Prospect of Rapid Growth in Environmental Damage

In a context of uncertainty, a seminal finding (Weitzmann, 1974) is that the best choice of policy instrument results from a comparison of the functions of external damage and of pollution abatement costs. If policy-makers presume *ex ante* that damage will increase greatly as pollution levels rise, or that there is a specific limit above which the damage will become unacceptable, it makes sense for them to set a constraint on quantities, as in the case of TPs. When they presume that pollution abatement costs will rise steeply as pollution levels are lowered, with damage remaining largely unaffected by short run variations in flows, there is an economic rationale for them to use a regulated price (a tax or a subsidy per unit abated), since this reduces the expected value of an error cost resulting from the choice of a non-optimal level for the policy target, relative to the choice of a quantitative constraint. This solution also serves to cap the unit amount that agents will be asked to pay for pollution abatement, thus making their costs more predictable. At the same time, if it is assumed that there are thresholds in the damage function or at least that this function has a steeply rising gradient, it is by choosing the quantitative rationing approach which will reduce the expected error cost (see Figure 7). In such a context preference should therefore be given to TPs rather than taxation.

As noted in Chapter 2, page 47, the fear of imposing excessive costs on economic agents may also lead policy-makers to adopt a mix of TPs and taxes for excess emissions or abstractions on permits holds. In this way, agents enjoy the specific advantages of TPs along with the assurance that they will not have to bear unit costs higher than the amount of the tax in order to meet their obligations, while also providing non-negligible guarantees regarding the level of physical performance to be achieved.

Diversity of the Economic Situations of Decentralised Agents

One of the principal advantages of the TPs is that they can take advantage of the information and actions of decentralised agents in a general context in which the individual circumstances of those agents are both diverse and contrasting. This advantage no longer exists if decentralised agents have no choice in practice over how to meet the constraints imposed (e.g. only one technical process can be used within the time limit imposed) or are in economically similar situations (same cost structures, same functions of pollution abatement costs). Moreover there may be increasing returns to scale from standardisation of equipment, together with simplicity of administrative management as the result of compliance with regulations requiring the use of specified processes.

Figure 7. **Uncertainty Effect Related to the Marginal Cost of Pollution Reduction**

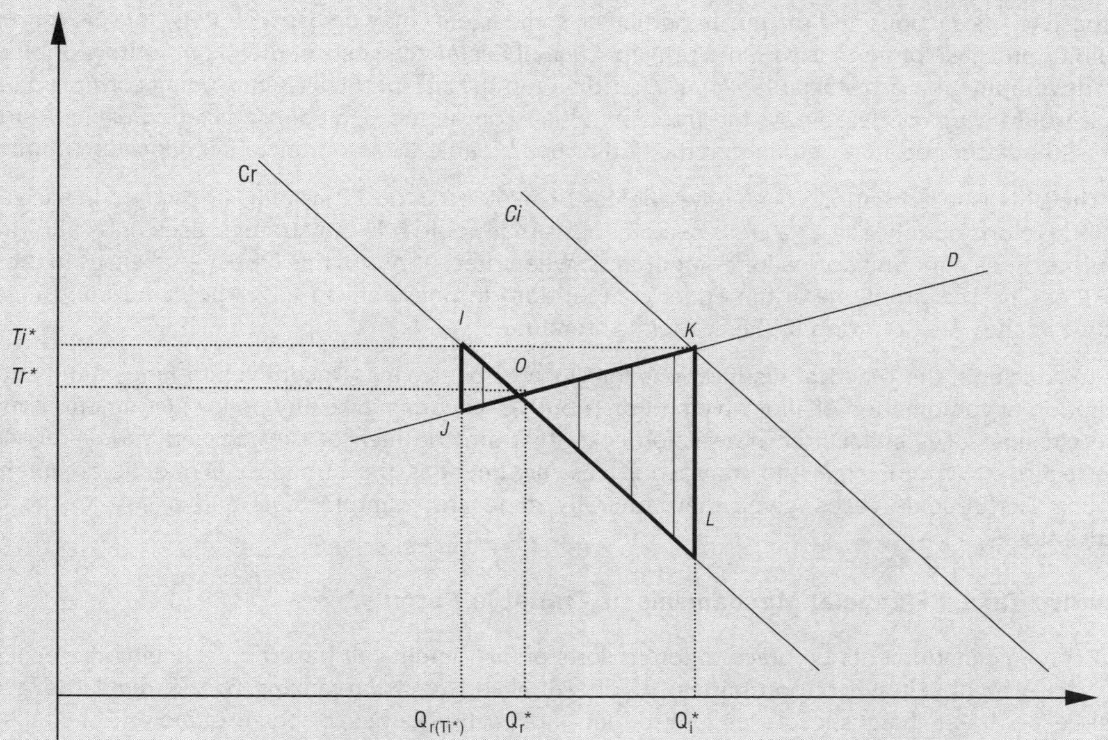

Opposite the **D** curve for marginal damage there are two curves for marginal cost of pollution abatement. **Ci** is the curve visualised by the authorities who have to decide on the choice of policy instrument and level of effort. **Cr** is the real curve, unknown to the authorities. In introducing a quantitative constraint, they would choose level **Qi*** as seeming to represent the optimum for the community. With a taxation approach, they would choose level **Ti***. In the case illustrated here, the expected value of the error cost is much smaller with the taxation approach (triangle **OIJ**) than with the quantitative constraint approach (triangle **OKL**). This is because the **C** slopes are much steeper than the **D** slope.

There are two riders to the conclusion that TPs lose their advantages in the circumstances just described:

- The description of the situation may be valid for the short term, but not for the longer term when technical innovation may broaden the range of options for action and when the economic situations of agents may differ. The relevance of the policy instrument chosen therefore depends on the time frame set. Is it a transitional measure covering a fairly short period (say five years) or does it constitute a long-term system?
- As noted in Chapter 2, page 33 and Chapter 3, page 69, a TP system may have the principal advantage of redistributing a scarcity rent among agents in a given population according to specific criteria of equity. This would seem to be the chief virtue of systems of transferable building rights (Renard, 1999).

Insignificant Risks of Market Power

From an economic standpoint, TPs are the best option if there is scope for the development of a properly functioning permit market, since transfers will be able to benefit from the economic efficiency of a competitive market. But this may not be the case if permit systems are used in an attempt to address local or sectoral problems involving a limited number of agents, all pursuing the same activity and therefore competing directly with one another in the product market, or agents in a highly asymmetrical position, some of them having a market power that allows them to adopt a strategic approach to transactions and pricing. In particular, some agents may devise a strategy for sale (or refusal to sell) or purchase of permits with the principal aim of raising the costs of their competitors or blocking their development (Sartzetakis, 1997*a*). Rather than run the risk of the system's being corrupted in this way, it would seem preferable, in the interests of fair competition, to choose taxation or non-tradable quotas, the latter option requiring that the authorities be able to determine a fair allocation of quotas.

The pitfalls just mentioned can nevertheless be avoided if the TP system is designed in such a way that it develops openly, say on a cross-sectoral basis that would rule out strategic uses or by allowing ad hoc procedures of permit access for new entrants. When precautions of this type are taken, as in the Acid Rain Program, the problems of imperfect competition do not seem to have the same importance in practice as they are accorded in the academic literature.

To conclude, the practical justifications for TPs are cost savings, incentives to innovation, and the separation or combination of allocative and distributive functions. Like any policy instrument, it may in some circumstances suffer from transaction costs that are too high or skewed and various economic imperfections. By and large, the transaction cost argument is the strongest economic argument for avoiding TPs in some cases, given that generally there are counteractants and offsets to the other disadvantages.

Incentive Taxes, Financial Mechanisms or Tradable Permits?

Economic instruments embrace different sorts of instruments all based on changing the economic context (price of relative opportunities) of decentralised decision-making of the regulated agents: subsidies, effluent charges, ecotaxes on products, abstraction duties, deposit-refund and the all scope of TPs. If the authorities wish to use economic instruments, there are three main options open:

- Incentive taxes which, by correcting prices, are designed to modify the usage behaviour of certain inputs or the emission of certain pollutants; to be effective, the tax basis must therefore be as close as possible to the behaviour responsible for the targeted environmental damage; from this standpoint, a tax on pollutant emissions that are rigorously monitored is much better than a lump-sum tax, a tax on inputs, or a tax on product sales.
- A financial mechanism which combines taxes or charges that will be paid into a special fund and subsidies from that fund to finance all or part of decentralised investments and operating costs of an environmental improvement or resource management programme. As in the case of the regulatory instrument, the economic efficiency of this mechanism will primarily depend upon the nature of criteria for the selection of projects to be subsidised and the quality of the technical and economic information that the organisation (agency, administration, consortium) managing the system can obtain with regard to the efficiency of the solutions put forward. The water agencies in France and the DSD (Duales System Deutschland) waste packaging recycling system in Germany are examples of how such mechanisms work.
- A TP system based on the introduction of quantified constraints and the uprising of a new market. In this case, the economic efficiency is derived from regulated agents taking the initiative to choose between abatement actions and making transfers in order to minimise costs.

What criteria might be used to choose between these three instruments? Incentive taxes and TPs are based on a price mechanism and are the two pillars which support economic instruments. However, the public authority does not introduce this mechanism in the same way in both cases. With a tax, the administration or a public agency makes an adjustment to market prices and allows a new equilibrium to emerge in the resulting quantities. With TPs, the administrative authority sets quantitative limits, while the performance of transactions leads to the formation of a market price that reflects the severity of the quantitative constraint imposed. In both cases, public intervention is required, which precludes any idea of a permit market developing spontaneously in the absence of public action. The two instruments exhibit major differences, particularly in a context of uncertainty, as noted in Chapter 4, page 88.

In economic terms, the choice is related to information, incentives, and organisational, transactional and redistribution costs. This means in particular that the designers of the new programme must pay particular attention to the informational structures of the rules of the game and the incentives they provide. For example, how is information shared between decentralised agents and the regulator? What type of transparency and honesty do the information-exchange procedures in place exhibit? What forms of behaviour do the rules adopted encourage?

Besides the question of information, the main arguments to be taken into account are as follows:

- *Secure the environmental performance.* If the authorities have a very poor understanding of how agents will respond to prices but have a clearer idea of the physical performance required, it would seem preferable to construct a regulatory system around the better known component, namely the physical performance targeted, which can pave the way towards TPs. In the same way, the very nature of the environmental or resource problem may matter. For instance, it may seem difficult to address specific local problems with national taxes, while regional or local TP systems may be more relevant.

- *Assess the aptitude to use existing services and capabilities.* In terms of organisational and transaction costs, it is important to determine whether existing departments (e.g. the tax authorities) would be able to assist in implementing the instrument chosen, or whether a new administration will have to be put in place. The same applies to the monitoring of the instrument, which would mean that the tax basis for the latter (emissions, inputs, equipment ratings, etc.) must be capable of being measured reliably.

- *Take into account the sensitivity of the regulated agents to price versus quantity signals.* The competitive structures in the regulated sector have an impact (see Chapter 3, page 56). Taxes are more appropriate if agents are sensitive to prices; in contrast, if the industry has an oligopolistic structure and product demand elasticity is low, it might be advisable to make use of non-transferable administrative constraints such as a requirement to reduce emissions by x %, to avoid strategic distortions.

- *Take into account the propensity, or reluctance, of the regulated agents to develop market transactions in the regulated field.* For various reasons (cultural, public image), external transactions on the market is not uniformly accepted as an appropriate regulatory tool for every type of problems. It also depends on national traditions. It would be useless to bet on TPs in contexts where regulated agents will not make use of transaction opportunities, even if this renunciation implies higher costs for them.

- *Consider the opportunity to achieve an ecological tax reform.* Both auctioned TPs and environmental taxes allow for fiscal reforms. Revenues may then be recycled in such a way to reduce economic distortions and social unbalances, or to pursue some distributive goals. This potential has to be considered before deciding which type of instrument should be chosen: what is relevant is the net economic impact of alternative instruments with or without fiscal adjustments.

- *Assess the distributive impacts.* Although theoretically the two instruments (taxes and TPs) are compatible with the full range of distributive options, there are implicit links between each instrument and a distributive strategy, so that distributive aspects play a key role in the political economy of the choice of an instrument. Firstly, in a standard incentive tax arrangement, the financial levy on agents, besides the desired incentive effect, generates a new resource that can improve the finances of the State or local authorities. In contrast, in a standard TP arrangement of the type that has been tried out in the United States, emission reduction credits or individual permit quotas are given to agents free of charge. It is for this reason that firms often perceive TPs as a means of avoiding taxes, while some administrations see them as an instrument that will deny them revenue from a new fiscal resource. Secondly, according to the structure of markets and price elasticities of the demand of goods upstream and downstream, agents directly participating to TP programmes may or may not have the opportunity to pass on their costs to other agents (suppliers, consumers). A complementary tax approach may allow public authorities to take these potential income effects into account by offering compensations to agents who will heavily bear the cost of environmental policy, in order to avoid unwanted income transfers from one category of agents to another.

Despite the advantages they both offer in terms of incentives and information, taxes and TPs remain less popular in practice than the regulatory approach based on technology. This discrepancy becomes easier to understand if the choice of an instrument of public policy is viewed in terms of problem-solving. It is only when TPs are able to offer novel advantages to the key actors in the decision-making process that they will stand any chance of being chosen. What this means is that reconciling the normative theoretical analysis and the positive empirical descriptions of the choice of policy instruments requires careful examination of the various stages in the design of new instruments on the basis of the problems encountered by the various types of actor involved in the policy process.

Chapter 5

Directions for the Development of a Transferable Permits System

Once the circumstances under which the use of TPs for the implementation of environmental policy might be appropriate have been determined, it still remains to determine which benchmarks should be used to design the instrument in practice. This is what this chapter sets out to do by recapitulating in the form of directions and recommendations the conclusions of the analyses and discussions put forward in the previous chapters. The first part of this chapter considers a selected number of strategic directions. These are the concerns and ideas that the designers of TP programmes must constantly bear in mind when making practical choices. The second part of the chapter addresses the way in which the process of designing a TP programme should be managed. Although this issues depends to a large extent on the rules of the art and the particular procedures followed by individual countries, the part this process plays in ensuring the success of the programme is so important that it merits a number of comments.

Strategic Directions for Determining the Nature of Transferable Permit Systems

Ensuring the Legal and Economic Security of Permits and the Adaptability of the Programme

Guaranteeing a high degree of security for TPs encourages agents to participate in transfers and helps to secure the expected gains in economic efficiency; it is therefore an important objective. At the same time a programme must be able to adapt to changed circumstances and in particular changes in information of a scientific nature. The priority must therefore be to seek to find solutions capable of reconciling these two objectives.

When transfers take the form of commercial transactions there is a considerable risk that trading will fall far short of the economic potential if the administrative rules could be suddenly changed or if allowance overshoots are not automatically penalised so that non-compliance costs more than attempting to comply with requirements by purchasing permits. It is particularly advisable to avoid revising the rules in a way that would lead to changes which might jeopardise the investments made previously or which might aggressively challenge the value of permits. It is therefore recommended that a stable framework and rules of the game be put in place in order not to create temporal inconsistencies in the choice of regulated agents.

Likewise, an effort must be made to avoid creating a static system of TPs at a time when new scientific information, new technological options or unforeseen development policies might legitimately prompt the competent authorities to seek to adapt the programme, for example, by establishing new objectives, by shortening the timetable for its introduction, by revising the levels of caps or minima or by extending its sectoral or geographical scope of application. It is therefore important to provide for the periodic revision of the ground rules. However, in order to allay fears that these revision phases might lead to arbitrary changes, it is recommended that the timetable, procedures and criteria for revisions be set out in advance.

A satisfactory compromise that reconciles permit security with programme adaptability may be secured as follows:

- *Build up the means of measuring or estimating the physical phenomena* targeted by the permits (e.g. SO_2 emissions from point sources, fish catches by fishing vessels): sensors, input or equipment accounting, tables of values for technical processes, etc.;

- *Devise an appropriate legal status for* TPs avoiding the shortcomings of both status of administrative authorisation and property rights; it is particularly advisable to clarify their status from the outset with regard to the rules applicable to firms' accounts and the applicable fiscal and tariff regulations;
- *Establish a full and credible set of financial penalties and sanctions* applicable to different levels of non-attainment on the basis of an economic and legal analysis of the question in respect of concerns relating to the integrity of the environment. It is necessary to distinguish between outright fraud or deliberate violation of rules, and modest and accidental overshooting of allowances. The former must carry penalties scaled according to degrees of likelihood or ease of detection, while the latter should be subject to sanctions proportionate to the maximum cost acceptable to the competent authority for the attainment of certain policy goals; the balance struck between the two will depend upon the sensitivity of the environment to the overshooting of limit-values or quotas and must not defined in the same way for all types of problem;
- *Guarantee stable rules for system operation and the initial allocation of permits at least over the medium term,* while at the same time, in the case of erratic fluctuations, adopting an approach whereby agents are not allocated absolute quotas but shares in a total quota valid for a given annual or multiannual period.
- *Specify beforehand the conditions under which the rules of the game may be changed* in terms of the timetable, changes in caps and baselines, rules for the allocation of individual quotas, and the extension of the programme to new categories of agent or to new types of pollutant.

Limiting Transaction Costs, Avoiding Unwarranted Obstacles to Transfers

If the aim of the authorities is to develop transfers in the form of commercial trading between individual economic agents, they must attempt to put in place a system which affords a wide variety of opportunities and which operates in a fluid and competitive way. Intermediaries such as brokers can play a positive role from this standpoint; however, it is only when there is a sufficient volume of transfers that brokers will decide to play a permanent role in this type of transaction. The authorities must also pay attention to the relationship between the average value of a transfer and average transaction costs in that too great a number of small transactions would generate costs that would be higher than the efficiency gains secured, even if use is made of modern electronic facilities[1]. A system that would involve several hundred operators at a regional or national level would be satisfactory, but even schemes involving a smaller number of larger participants can also yield good results, particularly if internal flexibility schemes supplement external transfers.

As far as possible, the system of prior authorisation for each projected transfer should be avoided. Experience has shown that this type of procedure can be a deterrent without being indispensable for meeting environmental objectives. The principle of prior authorisation should be applied only when this is really important to the environmental goals set, for example in approaches that make use of models to simulate flows of pollutant emissions dispersal and final impacts at the local level to determine the environmental acceptability of such pollution.

It is helpful to encourage the creation or involvement of trading exchanges to facilitate fair access to the market for all participants, ensure the broadest possible confrontation between supply and demand and thereby overcome the asymmetries in the information held by agents. Exchanges and other market intermediaries can also reduce search and trading costs and allow information to be made public on the market price of permits. When the volume of transactions is not big enough to justify bearing the fixed costs of a regular exchange, exchange-type mechanisms should nevertheless be aimed at to generate transactions that have efficiency features of a market. In some cases[2], consideration might be given, in order to maintain the economic effectiveness of the system, to granting a monopoly on transactions to a single mechanism of matching supply and demand for a given period of time or to concentrating the negotiation of transfers within limited periods of time. But in most cases, it might be advisable to allow for the existence of several transfer mechanisms and to make the transfer facility a permanent one, provided that transfers can be made in competitive and transparent conditions.

When determining the size of the area within which the TP system will be applied, it is important to ensure that it includes a sufficient number of potential participants. When the environmental impact depends on the location of pollutant emission or resource abstraction sources, there is always a trade-off between seeking to reduce total abatement costs and the acquisition of certainty as to the environmental performance obtained in each location. Once the cogency of the economic argument is recognised, defining geographical limits of possible transfers can no longer be confined to ecological considerations. If suitable equivalences cannot be defined, one can create parallel TP markets.

In a multi-goods context (different types of pollutant, different species of fish), it is relevant to try to find equivalencies that will enable these different elements to be incorporated into a single transfer scheme. This will increase transfer opportunities and extend the range of solutions open to agents, while reducing transaction and organisation costs.

Correcting Factors that Cause Distortion

Transfers, being the result of a decentralised initiative, make it possible to reduce the costs borne by the parties that make them. They also represent an advantage for the community, provided that the cost reductions do not have the effect of increasing environmental damage or the costs to third parties (local populations, consumers, taxpayers, other producers). Before introducing TPs, policy-makers therefore have to be sure that it will not have these negative repercussions and, if need be, make the necessary adjustments.

There would ostensibly seem to be two types of impact that should be avoided:

- *An increase in total environmental damage* due to the fact that the impacts of emissions or abstractions at different locations are not equivalent. This type of mismatch can be avoided either by establishing zones between which transfers are not allowed or by the use of offset ratios for inter-zone transfers.
- *Lending an unwanted direction to transfers* as a result of the fact that the parties concerned do not receive the same tax treatment for goods complementary to those involved in the transfers (e.g. excise duties on energy inputs). These differences in tax treatment may relate to the status of agents active either in the same sector (company-operated versus owner-operated fishing, for example) or in different sectors (water use by agriculture, industry or local communities; energy tax exemption for some activities and not for others). In situations where certain types of agent receive a more severe tax treatment and have higher abatement costs at the same time, transfers may spontaneously go in a direction opposite to the one that leads to increased collective efficiency in that the financial cost savings obtained through transfers by the parties concerned results in a loss of tax revenue for the State, which has to be borne by the population or taxpayers in the form of reduced public services or new taxes. At the same time, consumers, because of the inefficiency that has been introduced, will have to pay more for the products concerned than if the transfers had allowed the optimum choice to be made. This risk of distortion is obviously greater with international transfers between parties receiving very different tax treatments. But it also exists within domestic frameworks and should not be overlooked. This would be a new and special case of trade distortion due to marked differences between tax provisions.

If such distortions are significant, there are two possible types of remedy that can ultimately be considered: (1) the alignment of tax regimes and the challenging of arbitrary exemptions enjoyed by certain agents; (2) the introduction of territorial or sectoral restrictions on transfers with regard to the sources of distortion which have been identified and which it is assumed cannot be amended.

Encouraging Temporal Flexibility

The quantitative constraints applicable to TPs are generally introduced intermittently in stages several years apart. Without temporal flexibility, this approach causes arbitrary and costly jolts to the economy. The possibility of carrying forward permits valid for a given period to a later period during which more severe constraints will apply (banking) paradoxically encourages early cutbacks in emissions and enables operators to optimise their efforts over the whole span of periods. The outcome may be a more rapid improvement of the environment than that dictated by the constraints and a minimisation of total costs. Obviously, this type of flexibility must not present any threat to environmental and resource management goals by virtue of the scope it affords for concentration.

Circumstances are all-important here. It is clearly more difficult to regulate the population dynamics of exploited living species than to reduce long-range air pollution. In the latter case, the necessary guarantees can be supplied by adopting an appropriate stance towards the level of successive constraints and through regulatory regimes aimed at curbing local pollution in order to protect public health.

The main recommendations regarding time management of TPs are as follows:

- Authorise banking when there are no threats to environmental and natural resource management goals;
- Ensure predictability of the time path of constraints over a sufficient number of years; in many cases at least ten years must be allowed;
- Encourage operators to make forward transactions, or at least not prevent them from doing so;
- When activities proceed in multi-annual cycles, choose emission budgets valid for a period (say five years) which allows operators the widest margin of timing flexibility.

Adopting Procedures and Rules that Encourage Dynamic Efficiency and Innovation

The dynamic efficiency of a policy instrument lies in its ability to stimulate technical and organisational innovation to further the goals of the programme it is designed to implement, while preserving the conditions for efficient resource allocation across activities, branches and sectors. For quota systems, the initial allocation procedure is all-important. For credit systems, it is the technological frame of reference that counts.

Quota Systems

There are two issues to be considered: the system of initial allocation to existing facilities, and differences in treatment as between existing facilities and new facilities.

Finding Ways to Allocate Quotas to Existing Installations that Provide Suitable Incentives to Decision-Makers

Charge-free allocation of permits to firms with existing facilities or equipment (fishing vessels) imposes no direct financial load on those firms and preserves their financial capacity to make modernisation investments but may not give them strong incentives to promote any types of innovation. Innovations that will be quickly disseminated widely in their sector of activity are of no interest to them, since they will contribute to lower the value of the permits they hold. Their sole interest lies in specific innovations from which they alone could benefit. An analogous negative feed-back could take place if, through innovation, regulated agents contribute to reduce their future assignments of permits. On the other hand, an allocation by auction will give them a very direct incentive to innovate, in order to reduce their permit needs and the price to pay, or to maximise the profit derived from their production per TP held. Yet this auction procedure imposes a financial outlay that may impair their capacity to finance investment in new technologies if the capital market is tight and imperfectly accessible.

Consequently, if it is believed that the most favourable context for innovation is a combination of incentives to innovate and preservation of a sufficient financial capacity to do so, compromise solutions may be the answer. One would be to have free allocation for a share of the quota allowance (say 50%) and allocation by auction for the remainder. Another would be to allocate all permits by auction but to refund to firms a share of the proceeds on the basis of a criterion that is neutral in terms of incentive regarding environmental management strategies, such as the value added of the firms participating.

Avoiding Any Negative Effects of Differences in Treatment Between Existing and New Facilities

Traditionally, the regulatory requirements for new facilities are more stringent that those for existing facilities. Would it be wise to extend this asymmetry when putting in place a TP programme? This is what would happen if new facilities were to be made subject to a BAT-type procedure and at the same time obliged to acquire all the permits required for their activity in cases where existing facilities would benefit from a free allocation of TPs. At the same time, new facilities using up-to-date technology are generally less polluting on a unit emissions rate than existing ones, and need less permits per unit of output and so have a better competitive position than existing facilities. Here lies a trade-off that should be looked at with attention to avoid strongly asymmetrical conditions of competition between the two types of facility. If new facilities were to be penalised, new investments will be deterred and this might slow the plant renewal rate in the sector and therefore TP rules may act as a brake on innovation. If this risk is considered to be serious under the market conditions applicable in the sector considered, the danger might be allayed by reducing the regulatory gap between the two types of facility, one example being to limit the share of permits allocated free of charge to existing facilities.

Credit Systems

The possibility of earning tradable credits is an incentive to make further emission reductions and hence to seek out and apply the techniques that will permit this. It therefore encourages innovation and dynamic efficiency. However, it depends on the type of credit. If credits are awarded in relation with limits set in absolute terms, generally depending on maximum production capacity, it is likely that a proportion of the credits could be allocated for notional reductions that exist only on the paper in that firms rarely operate at theoretical maximum production capacity. There is therefore a systematic discrepancy between the average level of actual emissions and the theoretical maximum authorised. A windfall of this kind will have the effect of putting too many emission permits into circulation without any accompanying innovation. It may therefore be advisable, when allocating credits of that type, to adopt a more restrictive benchmark. This is a very delicate point in that firms are bound to argue that it is because of their past vigilance and innovation that they have succeeded in polluting less than they were authorised to.

The Process of Designing and Introducing Transferable Permits

Although in fact there are fairly few countries that have TP systems for pollution and natural resource management (water, fisheries, land use), it is not for want of proposals. In a number of countries (Norway, Switzerland and the United Kingdom, for example), projects have been designed and have sometimes even reached an advanced stage in the public decision-making process, stopping just short of the political decision binding governments and parliaments. In other cases, these proposals have resulted in the introduction of certain innovative provisions in existing regulations, at least on paper. But these provisions have either not been really applied or have given rise to such a small number of transactions that the arrangement has had scarcely any practical significance (Switzerland, Poland and France, for example).

There are two basic reasons for this state of affairs. One is the lack of a positive will to play the game of this instrument, or indeed resistance on the part of those who implement environmental policies or contribute to shape them. The other is a proliferation of constraints and difficulties created by the jungle of existing regulations. It is therefore advisable to place these constraints and difficulties within the broader context of the political economy of choosing environmental policy instruments. In many cases, if the move to TPs does not take place, it is not only because of obstacles that stand in the way, but also because of the absence of an impulse or a positive condition that is nonetheless required. Admittedly, there are social actors and population groups hostile to this instrument, for the reasons given in

Chapter 2, page 52, but this hostility is not the only explanation. Until recently there were many, in Europe and elsewhere, who did not know anything about TPs or else had formed a very approximate or distorted idea of them. Others thought that they were simply an oddity devised by the US environmental protection authorities, bearing no relevance to countries with different legal and political traditions (Cros and Godard, 1996).

Besides the clear identification of the obstacles to be overcome, there are two pre-requisites for the development of TPs. First, a positive movement must emerge (a need, will, project) involving a clear awareness among a sufficient number of actors that TPs can, better than other instruments, resolve the problems that affect the usual instruments or that the latter cannot resolve; second, it is necessary to set in motion a broader process of change with regard to the environmental administration. This concerns not only the relationships between government, enterprises and NGOs, but also the organisational culture of the actors on different sides who are involved in regulating the environmental protection field and the management of natural resources.

A Problem-Solving Approach to Raise Interest and Motivation Among Stakeholders

In order to bring order to the various factors that can affect the process of adoption of a policy instrument, the present section sets out to consider this process as the outcome of an application of the logic of problem-solving and coalition formation (Godard, 1998).

Rationale for Selecting Instruments and the Interplay of Actors

An important feature of the political economy of environmental decision-making is that economic efficiency, as understood by economists[3], is not a major concern of most of the actors involved in the process of designing and choosing a policy. Not that these actors are irrational. It is just that they each have their own objectives (see Box 19), while only a small number of players set themselves the aim of introducing a policy that will ultimately produce a satisfactory overall level of economic efficiency for the community.

Analysts and designers must accept the consequences of this state of affairs. It is therefore safe to say that an academic demonstration of economic efficiency resulting from the use of an instrument like TPs will not be enough to convince most actors to support its introduction. To win acceptance, the instrument has to be promoted as a response to the expectations and concerns of the principal actors who take part to the policy-making process. In other words, the design of a TP system must be framed within a problem solving approach related to the concerns of various stakeholders. As already noted, the first experiments with TPs in the United States were undertaken for fear that the economic development of certain areas would be blocked, not in pursuit of economic efficiency as such. A solution had to be found for that problem, while keeping within the general framework of the system set up by the *Clean Air Act*.

Box 19. **A Few Examples of the Concerns of the Actors Involved in Choosing a Policy Instrument**

Most of the prevailing concerns are usually fairly disparate and varied, for example: winning political support from certain social groups or organisations; achieving a noticeable advance in environmental protection or extending citizens' rights (as with the right to a healthy environment); obtaining a favourable redistribution of public resources (lower taxes); obtaining financial aid for a local project; acquiring greater influence on the political circles; gaining or maintaining control of financial resource allocation; hedging against protests from public opinion; mastering a new technology; securing new markets for domestic enterprises; seeing that a new policy instrument is compatible with the main legal rules in force and that administrative procedures are formally complied with; limiting the budgetary cost of a new policy, etc.

Obviously, whether or not TPs are the answer to agents' problems will depend on the nature of those problems. For example, if the problem of an NGO is how to achieve a definite improvement in environmental quality in a given locality, the possibility of permit transfers may be seen as a danger to be avoided rather than as a solution to be encouraged. Similarly, if the main concern of big industrial corporations is to acquire an exemplary green image in the eyes of consumers and NGOs, they will see the possibility of purchasing emission permits from other companies much more as a risk to be avoided than as an opportunity to achieve lower costs. On the other hand, if the main concern of industry is to protect itself against discretionary action by government and to counter attempts to raise tax pressure by way of green taxes and the like, pushing TPs can be appropriate strategy. The way in which the Acid Rain Program came about in the United States is a good illustration of the influences which the different players can bring to bear on this type of reform (Godard, 1994) (see Box 20).

Box 20. **What the Various Actors Found in the Acid Rain Program Adopted in the United States in 1990**

This programme was finally adopted after a long period of debate and controversy over the priority to give to this action and over the costs that would have to be borne by utilities, industry and consumers. The stalemate was ultimately resolved through a proposal to break with the conventional regulatory approach by establishing a market for SO_2 emissions. This proposal was drawn up on the initiative of an NGO, the *Environmental Defense Fund*, in collaboration with industry and the administration. Work on the proposal was then taken over by working parties set up by the *Center for Clean Air Policy*, which worked closely with Congress and in which both Republican and Democrat policy-makers worked alongside each other. Matters nonetheless remained uncertain until the last minute, amidst a fair degree of opposing opinions. The structure finally agreed upon for the programme was able to satisfy some of the concerns of the various groups in a position of influence with regard to the adoption of this TP programme.

The Republican administration of that time saw acid rain abatement as a way of improving its environmental image, which had been tarnished by its earlier action (attack on the EPA), and chose a type of instrument that could be promoted ideologically as a defence of market principles, combining freedom and efficiency with no danger of discretionary action and intrusion by government.

For the environmentalists, the programme promised new and steep reductions in acid deposition according to a strict timetable, notably with an overall cap on SO_2 and NO_x emissions and a specific cap for electricity generation. In return, they had to accept a degree of uncertainty about the geographic distribution of this improvement, which was a sticking point for some NGOs.

For the electricity companies and industry in general, the programme offered flexibility in the choice of means and all-round prospects of a significant reduction in the direct costs of pollution abatement. At the same time, the free allocation of allowances based on past performance (grandfathering) gave them assets that could be profitably sold or "banked". This effectively precluded any blocking coalition of those who stood to lose from a more stringent policy of pollution abatement.

Federal and State agencies for environmental protection were satisfied by the status-enhancing prospect of a new advance in environmental quality and by the promise of added means of administrative control: (a) continuous monitoring of power plant emissions; (b) a new system of administrative permits to operate for industrial units, a unique mandatory permit specifying all the different regulatory requirements as to safety and environmental quality which the units had to observe; and (c) new possibilities of initiative in the design of programmes for air pollution control.

For most local authorities, the new system promised an improvement in environmental quality without any shocks to the local economy and, most importantly, with no blocking of local economic development. Only the representatives of regions producing high-sulphur coal had reservations about a programme that would affect outlets for that product, whereas a compulsory but costly nation-wide programme of desulphurisation would have increased those outlets. The regions concerned received compensation in the form of additional emission allowances and specific aid for employees losing their jobs because of the programme for acid deposition abatement.

Members of Congress had opportunities, at the time of defining the rules of quota allocation, to advance the regional interests they represented. Some obtained additional allowances for key States capable of forming a coalition (Middle West, Florida).

Naturally, since the configurations of agents with an influence on public decision-making differ according to the types of problems and national situations involved, it is only to be expected that the institutional arrangements needed to support the TP system will likewise differ significantly from case to case. The many possible mixes of options for system design warrant this diversity.

Stages in the Adoption of a New Instrument for the Purpose of Problem Solving

To pave the way towards finding practical solutions, those responsible for designing and introducing new policies must ensure a favourable reception to a new instrument such as TPs. This means that they must treat the design of a new system in order to satisfy two requirements: make it an exercise in solving the various problems faced by the parties involved, but also fitting the general goals pursued by the new programme.

Broadly speaking, the process of instrument choice can be broken down into a series of logical steps. Those responsible for putting the new programme in place may wish to act directly or indirectly on some of those steps. At all events they must take them into account in their assessment of the situation. Their endeavour may fail as a result of the presence of obstacles or because certain conditions are not met.

1. *Actors of the policy-making process must become aware of the existence of problems not solved by the regulatory system in place or involuntarily caused by it.*

   The first obstacle to a reform is lack of awareness of the existence of problems posed or not resolved by the system in place. For example, the system may be judged satisfactory by its managers or by actors belonging to the "management community" responsible for the pollution or natural resources in question, because each gets something out of it. This does not mean that the problems are not there, but rather that they remain veiled until crises arise or else they are borne by unorganised actors who are not part of the "management community" such as local inhabitants and consumers.

   Thus the economic inefficiencies generated by many regulatory systems often go unnoticed, being accepted in effect by large numbers of agents not directly involved in the process of policy instrument choice. One of the great strategic contributions made by economic evaluations is that they publicly reveal the inefficiencies and squander generated by systems that nonetheless give satisfaction to those who operate them.

2. *The key actors in the existing system must become aware that they are already suffering or will suffer soon from the existence of these unresolved problems.*

   It may happen that the agents in environmental management know that the problems exist but this knowledge does not translate into a will for reform. This could be the case in two typical situations: (a) none of the key agents suffers from the absence of solutions, it is third parties (consumers, foreign populations, future generations, etc.) who are or who will be affected by these problems; (b) certain of the key agents who are affected negotiate individual solutions (waivers, special aid) with the authorities and manage to maintain their positions without improving the situation of unorganised agents (taxpayers, local populations), or even at the expense of the latter.

3. *It must be clear to agents that the existing system will be incapable of solving the problems by way of minor amendments and various accommodations.*

   Even if the problems (excessive costs, non-compliance and inadequate supervision, requirements not stringent enough to maintain or improve environmental quality, non-response to certain cases of pollution or certain risks, retrograde distributive effects, etc.) are now starting to be recognised, actors may still think that it is possible to improve things sufficiently by making a few minor adjustments to the existing system. The frequent belief of officialdom that it has the necessary information and competence to tell economic agents what new choices they should make is a major obstacle to the adoption of economically efficient policy instruments and TPs in particular.

Moreover, even when there is recognition of the need to introduce flexibility into a system corseted by all kinds of standards, agents often imagine that they can find an adequate solution through bilateral negotiations of a more or less informal character, either in order to determine the administrative prescriptions themselves or to define certain tolerances at the application stage. Flexibility through the negotiation of arrangements with the authorities, and not through reform, has been found attractive in a number of countries (Norway, Poland, France and Switzerland); recent widespread interest in voluntary agreements moves on the same wave.

The obvious disadvantages of this partial and informal approach to flexibility, sometimes flirting with non-application of the law, are that no environmental guarantees are provided and there is no prospect of reaching the economic efficiency that formal systems of flexibility like TPs can provide.

4. *Key actors must become convinced that* TPs *will be the best solution to the problems which concern them and of which they are now aware.*

   All sorts of obstacles may arise at this stage and put paid to plans to introduce TPs. This happens when there is still a wide gap between the nature of the problems, as agents perceive or visualise them, and at least some of the features of the TP system proposed. Potential difficulties include the geographical dimension (absence of guarantees as to local impacts, seemingly unsatisfactory definition of zones and equivalencies between damage in different zones); other distributive aspects, notably those related to the rules proposed for initial allocation; the perception of an ideological variance with the expectations of public opinion, and so on.

5. A *coalition of actors who share the same convictions regarding the need to change the system and the merits of* TPs *has to emerge in order to become the active advocate of policy change.*

   The absence of coalitions advocating TPs is fairly widespread. For cultural reasons or because of concern about their public image, the agents who stand to gain from supporting solutions of this type do not do so or are unwilling to invest in the organisational activities and lobbying needed to push the new arrangement through. In some cases, the potential advocates of policy change are a fragmented group unable to get themselves organised to promote a coherent proposal, as was the case in the United Kingdom (Steedman, 1999). In a political game that generally tends to involve three main categories of player between which local and national policy-makers must strike a balance, namely government, industry and environmental NGOs, it would seem that prior agreement between influential members of at least two of these categories is necessary to put through a reform. The recent experience of Norway bears out this observation (Schreiner, 1999) in that the use of TPs was only advocated by one of the players, namely industry. A proposal framed and supported by only one camp has very little chance of succeeding.

6. *The policy-making process succeeds in preventing the formation of a blocking coalition or neutralise it.*

   By virtue of greater organisational capacity and ability to represent economic and political interests, a minority group may often be capable of blocking a reform, as experience has shown in connection with the proposals for a carbon tax in European countries. This propensity depends on the forms of concentration or dispersion of the costs and benefits of the reform. If the benefits are dispersed over a large number of economic agents of low individual weight and the costs concentrated on a small number of firms or sectors with, say, financial power or political clout, there is a strong likelihood that a blocking coalition will emerge. It is then necessary to shape the proposal in such a way that those who have such blocking power can agree to adopt a neutral position if not become the beneficiaries of the reform envisaged. Proposals to allocate permits by auction will undoubtedly come up against a situation of this kind, which explains why that particular solution has not been put to much practical use in the environmental field despite the many advantages attributed to it by the theorists.

7. *The new policy instrument may rest on certain principles, concepts and pre-established institutional forms or on arrangements that can be regarded as precedents for* TPs.

   The legal approach focuses on precedents and case law. If the idea of TPs is completely new in relation to a country's institutional practices, this will certainly be an obstacle. On the other hand, if certain concepts and certain institutional forms are considered and referred to as precedents or bridgeheads for TPs, this should make the latter appear less of a radical novelty and more as an extension of practices already accepted by the legal establishment and also by most agents. Here, each country can draw on its administrative traditions and also on the most recent innovations in public services introduced over the past two decades in OECD Member countries.

8. *The profile of the new instrument must be consistent with the general trend of society, particularly as regards relations between State and civil society and the manner of approaching environmental issues.*

   Environmental polices are not a separate area of public policy-making and, more broadly, the functioning of society. An environmental reform has a greater chance of succeeding if it is consistent with the general trend of society (according to time and places, this can be a greater confidence in a decentralised approach that encourages the emergence of private rules, or in a market organised and regulated by government, or in administrative interventionism) and the main way in which the theme of the environment is treated.

   Are the issues primarily set as scientific (man as observer of the world), moral (the obligations of present generations to future generations and to nature), technological (solutions devised by technologists for technical problems), political (the sovereignty of states, to be challenged or preserved depending on the point of view; the transformation of North-South relations), or economic (recognition and efficient allocation of a new scarce resource by society as a whole)? TPs are tethered to physical constraints familiar and readily understandable to the community of natural scientists (physicists, ecologists, hydrologists) and engineers (technological know-how). They are also consistent with the economic approach, focusing on economic efficiency in the management of a scarce resource, and with that political approach for which freedom of decentralised choice and innovation are emphasised.

   Societies, be they national or local, which exclusively promote a moral or even sacred conception of the environment, and which emphasise standardisation and uniformity of behaviour along with management and control by government, are distinctly unfavourable settings for any plan to introduce TPs. If the latter are to succeed, permit trading must not be seen as an evil but extolled for the benefits it brings to all parties when conducted within a sound regulatory framework.

A Strategic Approach

The desire to incorporate the design of an instrument into the logic applied to the resolution of the problems perceived and faced by the various actors taking part in the policy-making process does not relieve those responsible for the design of the system from making a number of strategic decisions. These decisions primarily concern the scope of the programme, i.e. is the aim to overhaul the entire regulatory regime in order to promote fairly widespread use of TPs, to set up a separate and distinct system or to make the existing regime more flexible without undermining its bases? They subsequently concern the timing of application of the new instrument and, more precisely, the order in which the main components of the new system are to be introduced.

An Initial Choice of One of Three Options

There are three very different strategies towards the introduction of TPs: (1) to improve the economic efficiency of existing policies without disrupting the institutional framework; (2) to design a new framework that will remain separate from the routine activities of the environment administration and that is properly tailored to the way in which the instruments operates in order to address a specific problem; or (3) by reforming the entire regulatory framework and its conceptual basis.

These strategies call for diametrically opposed approaches to the institutional framework in place. Strategy (1) (improving the existing framework) first requires the determination of which components of the framework could be used to support instruments designed to provide greater flexibility, for example:

- Measurement and information networks covering the emissions or abstractions in question.
- Definitions of limit-values related to measurable performance and non process-specific.
- An autonomous regulatory agency and well-equipped and efficient enforcement services.
- Legal principles or forms that could serve as useful precedents for managing the introduction of permit transfers, notably as regards the legal status of the permits transferred. Particular attention should be paid to recent legal and administrative innovations, not only in environmental policy but also those relating to public regulation methods in the economic field and trends in the organisation of public services with the creation of independent authorities to regulate the new markets.
- The existence of a sufficiently extensive zoning plan to provide a suitable territorial framework for the introduction of instruments of flexibility.
- The existence of arrangements that in certain respects and to a certain degree prefigure the rationale of TPs: specification of block environmental requirements for an economic sector, firm or industrial site; arrangements based on the idea of transfer of obligations, as with the schemes introduced in France and Germany for recycling packaging waste (Sprenger, 1999; Buclet and Godard, 2000).

Strategy (2) (creation of a new framework tailored to TPs) must above all seek to identify within existing arrangements what elements, in terms of rules, procedures and concepts, must be avoided in the new system. The desire to avoid certain elements must be understood in the following two senses, namely that it is important to avoid:

- Making the new system subject to existing, but inappropriate, rules and procedures;
- Introducing defects into the new system that are similar to those observed in the current administrative system; for example, stringent regulations that focus on technology and that are based on a system of prior authorisation are not compatible with the widespread deployment of TPs.

A Political Pitfall to be Avoided

In terms of the political economy of the choice of instruments, consideration is often given to deploying systems of TPs once other approaches have already failed to achieve certain environmental objectives or when new political priorities, after a long period of delay, call for a sharp tightening of the constraints on activities responsible for resource abstraction or pollutant emissions. The background against which permit systems are introduced is therefore usually one in which requirements have become more stringent, which in itself will translate into an increase in the direct and immediate costs of the economic agents concerned and, in overall terms, the economic agents downstream.

This situation has a dual effect on the possibility of introducing a TP system. The prospect of a significant increase in costs increases the attractiveness of an instrument capable of minimising that increase. There is, however, a price to pay. The reasons advanced for increasing environmental constraints are usually opposed and contested in various quarters, particularly by industry which draws attention to the loss of competitiveness and jobs that will ensue. As a result, the context is not politically favourable to a broader review of previous practices associated with the regulatory approach. Since the administrative permits were not sold to firms, under the earlier regime agents merely had to contend with the expense of compliance with regulations, subject to a few small charges for administrative costs. To the extent that governments generally do not want the agents directly concerned by an environmental reform being totally opposed to that reform, existing experiences with such reform in which TPs play a part have all adopted the solution of an initial free allocation of permits[4]. In this way, there was no increase in the direct financial costs of firms compared with the increased burden they would have had under a regulatory approach.

Making wider use of TP granted for free as a basic component of policies towards the environment or the management of natural resources would be accompanied by major transfers of income away from consumers, who would have to pay more for the products offered, to existing firms receiving scarcity rents. The wider use of such schemes would also mean abandoning a policy of integrating ecotaxes into broader fiscal reforms (Majocchi, 1996; OECD, 1997; Bureau and Hourcade, 1998).

If the authorities want to be able to charge for permit allocation, and thereby find a way in which to avoid the political dilemma outlined above, it might be to their advantage to deal separately with the timetable for the introduction of three particular changes:

- The increased stringency of the environmental constraint (reduction of emissions, abstraction or capacities);
- The introduction of TPs;
- The change of rules giving access to TPs, away from a free allocation towards auctioning.

The financial impact of the reform on firms could thereby be staggered over time.

One possible course of action might be to start moving the regulatory regime towards an auctioned TP system without making any change to the level of environmental constraint. In a system applicable over a number of periods, introducing gradual increases (5%, 10% and then 25%) in the proportion of quotas offered for auction would ensure a transition that is not accompanied by the type of financial shock which precipitate crises. In the case of new problems, such as greenhouse gases, for which there is no specific policy already in place, a TP system could be introduced, for example, on the basis of allowances representing 100% of emissions over a reference period. It is only during a subsequent period, after ten or so years for example, that the stringency of environmental constraints would be increased.

Sequences of actions of this first strategy would nonetheless seem improbable. It would call for the ability to implement reforms *ab initio* without having to contend with pressure exerted by the problems to be solved or the political impatience on the part of certain social groups. The area of pollution control and that of the management of natural resources do in fact differ to this regard. Reforms in the area of pollution control are primarily aimed at improving the quality of the environment and are associated more or less closely with the management of emergencies or problems that are of great concern to certain of the parties concerned. It would scarcely be conceivable to undertake a reform which would only start to produce environmental benefits ten or so years down the line. With the management of resources such as fish stocks, the concern of governments, like that of the parties involved, is more often than not to improve the economic viability, and hence profitability, of activities whose rent had hitherto been dissipated through perverse competition based on free access to the resource. The policy aim in such cases is not to recover the rent for the benefit of the State or the community. The same is generally true as well for the agricultural use of water.

The opposite strategy is therefore *a priori* more credible, but nonetheless also poses problems. The reform starts by increasing the stringency of the environmental constraints and implements these constraints by introducing TPs allocated free of charge. Once the full regime has been achieved from an environmental standpoint, such as a permanent ceiling on emissions (as under the Acid Rain Program from the year 2010 onwards), the rule for allocating permits is gradually modified by increasing a growing share of permits allocated through an auction procedure. The political difficulty obviously lies in changing the rule for distribution after accepting initially to allocate permits free of charge. For this change to be possible, it is imperative that this two-phase evolution be made an integral and non-negotiable part of the initial reform and that this be clearly stated from the outset.

An alternative and perhaps neater solution would be to provide for a proportion of permits to be put up for auction at the very first stage of the process and for the sums raised through this auction to be remitted to participants. This would mean that three variables would have to be determined for each period: the share of permits allocated through auction and the share allocated free of charge; the share of the auction revenue to be remitted; the criteria governing the remittance of auction revenue to participants. The general aim of this scheme is to increase over time the share of permits distributed via the auction procedure, while at the same time decreasing the amount of revenue remitted to participants. These changes would nonetheless take place within a clearly established framework set out from the outset.

Facilitating the Acquisition of Experience

In many countries TPs remain an objet of intellectual curiosity unenlightened by any practical knowledge of them. It is advisable to give various types of actor an opportunity to get a practical experience of them and, with that purpose, to facilitate the task of programme designers at the regional or local level who wish to take initiatives of this kind.

One solution would be to permit, or even encourage, the deployment of small-scale programmes that are nonetheless valid applications of the instrument at either a local level (industrial basin, fishing zone, etc.) or a sectoral level (oil refining, etc.). These programmes would be aimed at acquiring initial experience and at testing various design principles that are currently contested, with a view to launching more ambitious programmes later. For such experimental programmes to be possible, in most cases a number of regulatory or institutional obstacles will have to be removed by making provision for exemptions to the general regulatory system in place.

On the basis of these experiences, it would be useful for the competent authorities to establish a general institutional framework prescribing the basic rules and procedures for TP programmes and a range of approved schemes like those devised by the United States Environmental Protection Agency (bubbles, offset, netting, banking).

Even if such moves were deemed premature in some countries, the authorities might nonetheless wish to prepare for the future by introducing changes to bring existing regulations more into line with the type of regulatory system needed for TPs. Three steps are of critical importance in this respect:

- A shift from regulations focused on technical processes (BAT, etc.) to the formulation of physical constraints on flows (emissions, abstractions, deposits) that are more in line with environmental objectives *per se* and that offer greater flexibility in the choice of means;
- A shift from environmental requirements expressed in terms of relative values of emission or abstraction flows to requirements expressed as shares of overall ceiling and absolute values (quotas);
- The assignment of responsibility for verifying policy implementation to independent administrative authorities whose long-term mission would be not only to ensure compliance with regulations but also to look after transfer activity and ensure fairness of transactions.

Notes

1. It should be kept in mind that part of transaction costs are not supported directly by the partners in a transaction but by the competent authorities, except in cases where the administrative costs are passed on in the form of administrative charges.
2. For example when the environmental constraints are such that the transfers which can be made at any time are contingent on transfers made earlier. Optimising transfers under such circumstances would call for the widest possible simultaneous confrontation between supply and demand.
3. In practice, the concept of economic efficiency boils down to two ideas: to act in such a way that total expenditure (not only that of government and industry) remains proportionate to the advantages it procures; to seek instruments that minimise the total cost to society (producers, consumers, government) in achieving a given environmental objective.
4. This is not the case in all areas. In the United States and several countries in Europe there is an auctioning procedure for the allocation of mobile telephone frequencies. The firms concerned accepted this procedure after considering the transaction costs and substantial delays that the development of an administrative scheme would have entailed.

Conclusion

For over twenty-five years now the research conducted by economists has demonstrated the gains of various types that contemporary societies can derive from greater use of economic instruments to achieve ambitious objectives in the area of environmental protection and the management of natural resources. Despite some remarkable advances, achievements to date remain well below the potential of such instruments while the environmental objectives pursued are becoming increasingly ambitious and moving ever closer to the heart of environmental objectives, development decisions and the choice of infrastructure. According to the aim of sustainable development, the goal is now to shift in a coherent way the main technical, social and institutional components of patterns of development. From environmental policies that simply brushed against the edge of the economic sphere, we have now come to reason in terms of sustainable development strategies, eco-efficiency or industrial ecology. There now exists an even more striking discrepancy between the objectives currently pursued and the type of instrument that is still primarily used in that the latter fail to offer the powerful and economically efficient incentives that would be needed to make goals that sometimes appear to be pipe-dreams into a reality.

The use of economic instruments that provide incentives such as taxes and TPs has suffered from the occasionally wide divergences between academic analyses, focusing on the theme of economic efficiency, useful for identifying the potential of such instruments, and the diverse individual concerns of the actors actually involved in shaping environmental policies. The priority now must be to narrow this gap, obviously not by abandoning the benchmark of economic efficiency but by paying renewed attention to the political economy of the choice of instruments. The aim is to secure a convergence whereby the instruments that are most effective in meeting certain environmental objectives and natural resource management goals can be converted into practical tools capable of being both the vectors of the solution to problems that empirical areas of action pose in the eyes of those involved in the "regulatory sphere".

TPs offer substantial scope for application in the most diverse of areas and not only in that of air pollution and fishery management, areas in which the largest number or the largest schemes currently exist. The regulation of building rights, waste recycling and recovery programmes, rationalisation of the use of deep water tables and even the protection of ecosystems are all areas in which TP programmes could be used to good effect.

This study has endeavoured to provide readers curious to learn more about an instrument which many actors still find novel a description of the main design options and the issues surrounding the choices that need to be made. It will have fulfilled its purpose if it prompts the reader to think in a new way about the approach to public policy and if it helps to dispel some misconceptions about an instrument that, while not a panacea, nonetheless represents one of the most interesting ways to significantly enhance economic efficiency and the effectiveness of environmental policies.

Bibliography

ADAMS, J. (1997), "Globalisation, Trade and Environment", in OECD, *Globalisation and Environment – Preliminary Perspectives*, OECD, Paris.

AMANN, M., FORSUND, F. and KLAASSEN, G. (1994), "Emissions trading in Europe with an exchange rate", *Environmental and Resource Economics*, **4**. pp. 305-330.

BAILEY, P., GOUGH, C. and MILLOCK, K. (1994), "Sulphur emission exchange rates", in F. Forsund and G. Klaassen (eds), *Economic Instruments for Air Pollution Control*, Dordrecht, Kluwer.

BAILEY, P. and JACKSON, T. (1999), "Joint implementation for controlling sulphur in Europe and possible lessons for carbon dioxide", in S. Sorrell and J. Skea (eds), *Pollution for sale. Emissions trading and joint implementation*, Cheltenham, Edward Elgar, pp. 255-271.

BOHI, D.R. and BURTRAW, D. (1997), SO_2 *Allowance Trading: How Experience and Expectations Measure Up*, Washington DC, Resources for the Future, Discussion Paper 97-24, February, 21 p.

BOHM, P. (1999), "An emission quota trade experiment among four Nordic countries", in S. Sorrell and J. Skea (eds), *Pollution for sale. Emissions trading and joint implementation*, Cheltenham, Edward Elgar, pp. 299-321.

BUCLET, N. and GODARD, O. (eds.) (2000), *Municipal Waste Management in Europe – A Comparative Study in Building Regimes*, Dordrecht & London, Kluwer.

BUREAU, D. and HOURCADE, J.-C. (1998), "Les dividendes économiques d'une réforme fiscale écologique", in Conseil d'analyse économique auprès du Premier Ministre, *Fiscalité de l'environnement*, Paris, La Documentation française, pp. 41-81.

BURTRAW, D. (1996), "The SO_2 emission trading program: cost savings without allowance trades", *Contemporary Economic Policy*, 14, (2) pp. 79-94.

CASON, T.N. (1993), "Seller incentive properties of EPA's emission trading auction", *Journal of Environmental Economics and Management*, 25, pp. 177-195.

COASE, R.H. (1960), "The problem of social cost", *Journal of Law and Economics*, III, October, pp. 1-44.

CRAMTON, P. and KERR, S. (1998), *Tradable carbon allowance auctions: how and why to auction*, Washington DC, Center for Clean Air Policy, March.

CROCKER, T.D. (1996), "The structuring of Atmospheric Pollution Control Systems", in H. Wolozin (ed.), *The Economics of Air Pollution*, New York, W.W. Norton.

CROS, C. (1999), "Public policy and institutional trajectories: what about introducing SO_2 trading in France?", in S. Sorrell and J. Skea. (eds), *Pollution for sale. Emissions trading and joint implementation*, Cheltenham, Edward Elgar, pp. 154-169.

CROS, C. and GODARD, O. (1996), *Trajectoires institutionnelles et choix des instruments de politique publique. Les marchés de droits à polluer aux Etats-Unis et en France. Le cas de la pollution atmosphérique*, Paris, CIRED, Report for the "Future studies and scientific watch" programme run by the French Ministry of the Environment, January.

CROS, C. and GODARD, O. (1998), "The economic design of a potential tradable permit system for SO_2 emissions in the European Union", *European Economy – Reports and studies series* (1), European Commission, Directorate General for Economic and Financial Affairs, pp. 91-127.

DALES, J.H. (1968*a*), *Pollution, Property and Prices*, Toronto, Toronto University Press.

DALES, J.H. (1968*b*), "Land, water and ownership", *Canadian Journal of Economics*, 1, (4), November, pp. 791-804.

DEMSETZ, H. (1964), "The Exchange and Enforcement of Property Rights", *Journal of law and economics*, 7 (11).

DENTE, B. (ed.), *Environmental Policy in Search of New Instruments*, Dordrecht, Kluwer.

DWYER, J.P. (1992), "Chapter 3. California's Tradeable Emissions Policy and its Application to the Control of Greenhouse Gases: A Case Study", in *Climate Change: Designing a Tradeable Permit System*, Paris, OECD, pp. 41-80.

ELLERMAN, D., SCHMALENSEE, R., JOSKOW, P., MONTERO, J.P., BAILEY, E.M. (1997), *Emissions trading under the U.S. Acid Rain Program. Evaluation of compliance costs and allowance market performance*, Cambridge, Center for Energy and Environmental Policy Research, MIT, October, 77 p.

FALQUE, M. and MASSENET, M. (dir.) (1997), *Droits de propriété et environnement*, Paris, Dalloz.

FORSUND, F. and KLAASSEN, G. (eds) (1994), *Economic Instruments for Air Pollution Control*, Dordrecht, Kluwer.

GADGIL, M. and RAO, P.R.S. (1994), "A system of positive incentives to conserve biodiversity", *Economic and political weekly*, August 6, pp. 2103-2107.

GODARD, O. (1993*a*), "Chapter 2. Taxes", in *International Economic Instruments and Climate Change*, Paris, OECD, pp. 43-101.

GODARD, O. (1993*b*), "Stratégies industrielles et conventions d'environnement: de l'univers stabilisé aux univers controversés", *INSEE-Méthodes*, (39-40), December, pp. 145-174.

GODARD, O. (1994), *L'expérience américaine des permis négociables dans le domaine de la pollution atmosphérique*, Paris, CIRED, (Coll. Environnement et Société 94/11), December, 92 p.

GODARD, O. (1995*a*), "Trajectoires institutionnelles et choix d'instruments pour les politiques d'environnement dans les économies en transition", *Revue d'études comparatives Est-Ouest*, 26 (2), CNRS, June, pp. 39-58.

GODARD, O. (1995*b*), *Théorie et pratique de la mise en oeuvre du Principe Pollueur-Payeur*, Paris, SMASH, Report submitted to the DGAD/SRAE of the French Ministry of the Environment, July.

GODARD, O. (1998), "Understanding policy and institutional obstacles to the adoption of domestic tradable permits: a simple model", *Workshop on Domestic Tradable Permit Systems for Environmental Management: Issues and Challenges*, Paris, OECD, 24-25 September.

GODARD, O. (1999), "Chapter 15. Economic instruments and institutional constraints: possible schemes for SO_2 emissions trading in the EU", in S. Sorrell and J. Skea. (eds), *Pollution for sale. Emissions trading and joint implementation*, Cheltenham, Edward Elgar, pp. 272-295.

GODARD, O. (1999) and HENRY, C. (1998), "Les instruments des politiques internationales de l'environnement : la prévention du risque climatique et les mécanismes de permis négociables" in Conseil d'analyse économique auprès du Premier Ministre, *Fiscalité de l'environnement*, Paris, La Documentation française, July, pp. 83-174.

HAHN, R.W. (1984), "Market power and transferable property rights", *The Quarterly Journal of Economics*, November, pp. 753-763.

HAHN, R.W. and HESTER, G.L. (1989*a*), "Where did all the markets go? An analysis of EPA's Emissions Trading Program", *Yale Journal on Regulation*, 6, (1), Winter, pp. 109-153.

HAHN, R. and HESTER, G.L. (1989*b*), "Marketable permits: Lessons for theory and practice", *Ecology Law Quarterly*, 16, (2), pp. 361-406.

HAHN, R. and NOLL, R. (1982), "Designing a market for tradeable emission permits", in W.A. Magat (ed.), *Reform of Environmental Regulation*, Cambridge (Mass.), Ballinger, pp. 119-146.

HARRISON, D. (1994), *The distributive effects of economic instruments for environmental policy*, Paris, OECD.

HARRISON, D. (1999), "Tradable Permits for Air Pollution Control: the United States Experience", in *Implementing Domestic Tradable Permits for Environmental Protection*, Paris, OECD, pp. 23-51.

HØIBYE, G. (1999), "Designing a scheme for SO_2 trading in Norway", in S. Sorrell and J. Skea. (eds), *Pollution for sale. Emissions trading and joint implementation*, Cheltenham, Edward Elgar, pp. 101-123.

HOURCADE, J.C. and BARON, R. (1993), "Chapter 1. Tradeable permits", in *International Economic Instruments and Climate Change*, Paris, OECD, pp. 11-44.

HOURCADE, J.C., RICHELS, R. and ROBINSON, J. *et al.* (1997), "Chapter 8. Estimation des coûts de limitation des émissions de gaz à effet de serre", in J.P. Bruce, H. Lee H. et E.F. Haites (dir.), *Le changement climatique. Dimensions économiques et sociales. Contribution du groupe de travail III au Deuxième rapport d'évaluation du Groupe d'experts intergouvernemental sur l'évolution du climat*. Paris, Editions 4D, distributed by La Documentation française, pp. 277-315.

HOWE, C. (1994), "Taxes versus tradeable discharge permits: A review in the light of the US and European experience", *Environmental and Resource Economics*, 4 (2), April, pp. 151-169.

VAN IERLAND, E.C., KRUITWAGEN, S. and HENDRIX, E.M.T. (1994), "Tradable Discharge Permits for Acidifying Emissions in Europe: 'guided' bilateral trade" in F. Forsund and G. Klaassen (eds), *Economic Instruments for Air Pollution Control*, Dordrecht, Kluwer.

JEANRENAUD, C. (1999), "Obstacles to the implemenation of tradable permits: lessons from recent projects – The case of Switzerland" in *Implementing Domestic Tradable Permits for Environmental Protection*, Paris, OECD, pp. 167-182.

JOHNSTONE, N. (1999*a*), "Tradable permit systems and industrial competitiveness: A review of issues and evidence", in *Implementing Domestic Tradable Permits for Environmental Protection*, Paris, OECD, pp. 221-252.

JOHNSTONE, N. (1999*b*), *Permit Allocation Methods, Greenhouse Gases, and Competitiveness*, Paris, OECD, ENV/EPOC/GEEI(99)1.

JOSKOW, P. and SCHMALENSEE, R. (1997), "The political economy of market-based environmental policy: The US Acid Rain Program", *Journal of Law and Economics*.

KETE, N. (1992), "Chapter 4. The US Acid Rain Control Allowance Trading System", in OECD, *Climate change. Designing a tradeable permit system*, Paris, OECD Publications, pp. 69-93.

KLAASSEN, G. (1996), *Acid Rain and Environmental Degradation. The Economics of Emissions Trading*, Edward Elgar.

KOUTSTAAL, P. (1997), *Economic Policy and Climate Change. Tradable Permits for Reducing Carbon Emissions*, Cheltenham, Edward Elgar.

KRAEMER, R.A. and BANHOLZER, K.M. (1999), "Tradable permits in water resource management and water pollution control", in *Implementing Domestic Tradable Permits for Environmental Protection*, Paris, OECD, pp. 75-107.

MAJOCCHI, A. (1996), "Green fiscal reform and employment: A survey", *Environmental and Resource Economics*, 8 (4), December.

MONTGOMERY, W.D. (1972), "Markets and Licences and Efficient Pollution Control Programs", *Journal of Economic Theory*, 5 (4), December, pp. 395-418.

MULLINS, F. (1997), *Lessons from existing trading systems for international GHG emission trading. Paper 1: The US Acid Rain Program: SO_2 Allowance Trading*, Paris, Expert paper by the OECD and IEA secretariats for the Annex 1 Expert Group on the UN FCCC, April, 11 p.

NORDIC COUNCIL OF MINISTERS (1997), *A joint implementation as emission quotas trades. An experiment among 4 Nordic countries*, Copenhagen, (1997.4).

NUSSBAUM, B.D. (1992), "Chapter 2. Réduction progressive du plomb dans l'essence aux Etats-Unis. Réglementations, incitations, échange et capitalisation" in OECD, *op.cit.*, pp. 21-34.

OECD (1975), *The Polluter-Pays Principle. Definition, analysis, implementation*, Paris, OECD.

OECD (1992), *Climate change. Designing a tradeable permit system*, Paris, OECD.

OECD (1997), *Environmental taxes and green tax reform*, Paris, OECD.

OECD (1999*a*), *Implementing Domestic Tradable Permits for Environmental Protection*, Paris, OECD.

OECD (1999*b*), *Voluntary Approaches for Environmental Policy in OECD Countries: An Assessment*, Paris, OECD.

O'NEIL, W., DAVID, M., MOORE, C., JOERES, E. (1983), "Transferable Discharge Permits and Economic Efficiency: The Fox River", *Journal of Environmental Economics and Management*, 10, pp. 346-355.

OSTROM, E. (1990), *Governing the Commons. The Evolution of Institutions for Collective Action*, Cambridge, Cambridge University Press.

PEARSE, P.H. (1980), "Property rights and the regulation of commercial fisheries", *Journal of Business Administration*, 11 (1-2), pp. 185-209.

PEARSE, P.H. (ed.) (1982), *Turning the Tide: A New Policy for Canada's Pacific Fisheries. Final report of the Commission for Pacific Fisheries Policy*, Vancouver, Department of Fisheries and Oceans.

PEARSE, P.H. (1992), "Developing property rights as instruments of natural resources policy. The case of the fisheries", in OECD, *Climate change. Designing a tradeable permit system*, Paris, OECD.

RÉMOND-GOUILLOUD, M. (1989), *Du droit de détruire. Essai sur le droit de l'environnement*, Paris, PUF.

RENARD, V. (1999), "Application of tradable permits to land-use management", in *Implementing Domestic Tradable Permits for Environmental Protection*, Paris, OECD, pp. 53-73.

ROBERTS, M. and SPENCE, M. (1976), "Effluent charges and licences under uncertainty", *Journal of Public Economics*, 5, April/May, pp. 193-208.

RUBIN, J. (1993), *Marketable Emission Permit Trading and Banking for Light-Duty Vehicle Manufacturers and Fuel Suppliers*, PhD Dissertation UCD-ITS-RR-93-20, Davis, University of California.

SARTZETAKIS, E.S. (1994), "Permis d'émission négociables et réglementation dans des marchés de concurrence imparfaite", *L'Actualité économique*, 70 (2), June, pp. 139-157.

SARTZETAKIS, E.S. (1997*a*), "Raising rivals' costs strategies via emission permits markets", *Review of Industrial Organization*.

SARTZETAKIS, E.S. (1997*b*), "Tradeable emission permits regulations in the presence of imperfectly competitive product markets: Welfare implications", *Environmental and Resource Economics*, 9, pp. 65-81.

SCHREINER, P. (1999), "Obstacles to the implementation of tradable permits: The case of Norway", in *Implementing Domestic Tradable Permits for Environmental Protection*, Paris, OECD, pp. 127-145.

SCHWARZE, R. and ZAPFEL, P. (2000), "Sulfur Allowance Trading and the Regional Clean Air Incentives Market: A Comparative Design Analysis of Two Major Cap-and-Trade Permit Programs," *Environmental and Resource Economics*, 17 (1), August.

SKEA, J. (1999), "Chapter 19. Flexibility, emissions trading and the Kyoto Protocol", in S. Sorrell and J. Skea (eds), *Pollution for sale. Emissions trading and joint implementation*, Cheltenham, Edward Elgar, pp. 299-321.

SMITH, S. (1999), "The compatibility of tradable permits with other environmental policy instruments", in *Implementing Domestic Tradable Permits for Environmental Protection*, Paris, OECD, pp. 199-219.

SORRELL, S. and SKEA, J. (eds) (1999), *Pollution for sale. Emissions trading and joint implementation*, Cheltenham, Edward Elgar.

SORRELL, S. (1999), "Why sulphur trading failed in the UK", in S. Sorrell and J. Skea (eds), *Pollution for sale. Emissions trading and joint implementation*, Cheltenham, Edward Elgar., pp. 170-207.

SPRENGER, R.U. (1999), "Designing a scheme for trading non-returnable beverage containers in Germany", in S. Sorrell and J. Skea (eds), *Pollution for sale. Emissions trading and joint implementation*, Cheltenham, Edward Elgar, pp. 299-321.

STAVINS, R. (1995), "Transaction costs and tradeable permits", *Journal of Environmental Economics and Management*, 29 (2), September, pp. 133-148.

STEEDMAN, J. (1998), "The case of the UK: Sulphur permit quota switching", in *Implementing Domestic Tradable Permits for Environmental Protection*, Paris, OECD, pp. 183-195.

TIETENBERG, T.H. (1985), *Emissions Trading. An Exercise in Reforming Pollution Policy*, Washington DC, Resources for the Future.

TIETENBERG, T.H. (1992), *Environmental and Natural Resource Economics*, New York, HarperCollins Publications.

TONNESSEN, J.N. and JOHNSEN, A.O. (1982), *The History of Modern Whaling*, Canberra, Australian University Press.

TVERSKY, A. and KAHNEMANN, D. (1981), "The framing of decisions and the psychology of choice", *Science*, 211, pp. 453-458.

VICKREY, W. (1961), "Counterspeculation, auctions and competitive sealed tenders", *Journal of Finance*, 16, pp. 8-37.

WALLIS, P. (1998), "Transferable fishing quotas: Experience in OECD countries", in *Implementing Domestic Tradable Permits for Environmental Protection*, Paris, OECD, pp. 109-124.

WEITZMANN, M.L. (1974), "Prices versus quantities", *Review of Economic Studies*, 41, pp. 477-491.

WESNEY, D. (1988), "Applied fisheries management plans: Individual transferable quotas and input controls", *The Scientific Foundations of Right Bases Fishing Workshop*, Reykjavik, 27 June to 1 July.

WILLIAMSON, O. (1985), *The Economic Institutions of Capitalism. Firms, Markets, Relational Contracts*, New York, The Free Press.

ZAPFEL, P. (2000), "Negotiated agreements and 'flexible mechanisms': building blocks for efficient Kyoto implementation strategies in the European Union?", in K.L. Brockmann and M. Stronzik (eds), *Flexible Mechanisms for an Efficient Climate Policy: Cost Saving Policies and Business Opportunities*, Heidelberg, Physica-Verlag, (ZEW Economic studies 11), pp. 87-98.

ZYLICZ, T. (1999), "Obstacles to implementing tradable pollution permits – The case of Poland", in *Implementing Domestic Tradable Permits for Environmental Protection*, Paris, OECD, pp. 147-165.

OECD PUBLICATIONS, 2, rue André-Pascal, 75775 PARIS CEDEX 16
PRINTED IN FRANCE
(97 2001 07 1 P) ISBN 92-64-18656-5 – No. 51855 2001